TWAYNE'S WORLD AUTHORS SERIES

A Survey of the World's Literature

Sylvia E. Bowman, Indiana University

GENERAL EDITOR

TWAYNE'S WORLD AUTHORS SERIES (TWAS)

The purpose of TWAS is to survey the major writers —novelists, dramatists, historians, poets, philosophers, and critics—of the nations of the world. Among the national literatures covered are those of Australia, Canada, China, Eastern Europe, France, Germany, Greece, India, Italy, Japan, Latin America, the Netherlands, New Zealand, Poland, Russia, Scandinavia, Spain, and the African nations, as well as Hebrew, Yiddish, and Latin Classical literatures. This survey is complemented by Twayne's United States Authors Series and English Authors Series.

The intent of each volume in these series is to present a critical-analytical study of the works of the writer; to include biographical and historical material that may be necessary for understanding, appreciation, and critical appraisal of the writer; and to present all material in clear, concise English—but not to vitiate the scholarly content of the work by doing so.

Guillén de Castro

By WILLIAM E. WILSON

University of Washington

Twayne Publishers, Inc. :: New York

To
Naomi Steil
My favorite University student
who for many years has been
Naomi Steil Wilson

Preface

The writer of a book about a major prolific author has considerable freedom in the way in which he treats his subject. In the
case of Cervantes, for example, the approach can be limited to
the biographical, since the life of Cervantes has so much of the
dramatic about it. Another possibility would be a book which
deals with the ways in which various generations, literary schools,
and authors have interpreted Cervantes' great novel *Don Quijote
de la Mancha*. But the writer of a book about a minor and yet
a quite important author such as Guillén de Castro (1569–1631)
finds himself limited to a considerable degree. The biographical
approach would have minor appeal, and a book only about his
plays, scarcely more than thirty in number, would be of interest
to only a small number of specialists. The present study is not
intended primarily for specialists. It is intended, rather, for students of Spanish who are in the early stages of their study of the
drama of Spain's Golden Age (1550–1681), and for readers in
general, especially those who are interested in acquiring some
knowledge of this dramatist whose play *Las mocedades del Cid*
(*The Youthful Deeds of the Cid*) was the inspiration for Pierre
Corneille's *Le Cid,* the first great French Classic tragedy or tragi-
comedy, as some prefer to call it.

In this study Castro's plays will be used as a nucleus around
which certain important aspects of the literature of the period
will be introduced. For in spite of the rather small number of his
plays, Guillén de Castro does have much to tell us about Golden
Age literature. The chapter on his versification and the dating of
his plays, for example, is intended to help toward an introduction to Spanish prosody. In his incorporation of Spain's rich ballad
lore, he is second only to the great dramatist Lope de Vega. His
use of this material is dealt with in connection with his sources,
and especially in the long chapters which deal with the Cid in

history, in the chronicles, and in literature. The inclusion of parallel columns gives a graphic view of the way in which Castro utilized the ballads. This method of presentation should be welcomed by many who have read about his extensive use of these poems, but who have until now lacked the opportunity to see it presented in this manner. Castro gives us at least an adequate picture of his nation's peculiar code of honor, a code which one critic has called "perverted idealism." In his play *El perfecto caballero* (*The Perfect Knight*) and elsewhere, he takes up the Spanish concept of what a nobleman's background and conduct should be, a concept which differs in certain respects from the Italian, French, and English views which prevailed during the sixteenth and seventeenth centuries. The affected or manneristic literary style which characterizes a great deal of the literature of the Baroque period is dealt with in the chapter on technique. The study closes with a discussion of Castro's influence upon dramatists of his age, followed by a summary of several recent scholarly contributions based chiefly upon his two *Cid* plays.

I should like to express my gratitude to Professor Gerald E. Wade for many valuable comments and for help in securing material not available at the University of Washington.

WILLIAM E. WILSON

Seattle, Washington

Contents

Contents

Chronology

1569   Guillén de Castro was born in Valencia, Spain.

1592   He became a member of the *Academia de los Nocturnos* in Valencia.

1593   He served as captain in the Coast Guard to defend against attacks by Moorish pirates. In this same year Castro was involved in an unsavory lawsuit with a certain Helena Fenollar.

1595   He married doña Marquesa Girón de Rebolledo, who died probably before 1600.

1602   He received a prize in Valencia for a poem written in honor of St. Raymond of Peñafort.

1607   He was appointed governor of Scigliano, Italy, by the Count of Benavente, don Juan Alonso Pimentel de Herrera, Captain General of Naples.

1608   Two of his plays, *El caballero bobo* (*The Foolish Young Gentleman*) and *El amor constante* (*Constant Love*), were published in a volume of twelve plays by four Valencian dramatists.

1609   The Count of Benavente granted him a leave of absence to return to Valencia, where he joined the expedition which was to transfer the Moriscos expelled from the province to North Africa.

1610   He received permission to remain in Spain for one year without pay, instead of returning to Scigliano. He was apparently suffering illness.

1611   His successor was appointed to the governorship of Scigliano.

1613   Castro returned to Italy, his illness apparently having lasted from 1610 until this year.

1616   Back in Valencia, he organized the *Academia de los montañeses del Parnaso*.

1618   His first volume of plays was published in Valencia. He probably went to Madrid during this year.

1619   His patron, don Juan Téllez Girón, deeded a parcel of land to him.

1621   The second printing of his first volume of plays was issued in Valencia.

1623   He mortgaged the property deeded to him by his patron. He returned to Valencia.

1624   Castro was accused of bribing a criminal to murder a nobleman, but the matter was not pressed.

1625   His second volume of plays was published in Valencia.

1626   He returned to Madrid, where he married doña Angela Salgado, a member of the household of his patron.

1631   He died in Madrid.

CHAPTER 1

Castro's Life and Works

I Biographical Sketch

GUILLÉN de Castro y Bellvis was born in Valencia in 1569. According to local legends, he could trace his descent on his father's side to Laín Calvo, an early judge of Castile and reputed grandfather of Rodrigo Ruy Díaz de Vivar, the famed Cid Campeador. This could indeed explain Castro's interest in that well-known hero of Spain. On his mother's side, Castro was descended from King John I of Aragon.

The atmosphere of Valencia in the latter half of the sixteenth century was ideal for a budding dramatist like Guillén de Castro. One of the leading cities of Spain from the point of view of arts and letters, Valencia was the home of several prominent dramatists, among them Rey de Artieda, Francisco Tárrega, Cristóbal de Virués, and Gaspar de Aguilar. Young Castro also had the opportunity to come into contact with Lope de Vega, who, having been banished from Madrid in 1595 because of a duel, lived in Valencia between that date and 1597. Lope returned to Valencia in 1599 when Philip II married Margarita of Austria in that city. A recent work on the Valencian dramatists indicates that they exercised considerable influence on Lope de Vega.[1]

In 1592 Castro became a member of the *Academia de los Nocturnos* (*Literary Society of the Night Revelers*), a society which had been founded in Valencia in 1591. Meetings were held every Wednesday evening, which explains the name of the society; the sessions were given over to "an almost identical distribution of devout and scabrous material."[2] Castro's name as a member of the society was "Secreto," and during 1592 and 1593 he contributed twenty-five poems and four prose compositions as his share of the proceedings.[3] The activities of the *Academia de los Nocturnos* came to an end in 1594, but despite its short duration, it was the most important Spanish literary society outside Madrid,

13

and was the equal of many similar societies in the Spanish capital itself.[4]

Further evidence of Castro's interest in literary matters is found in his participation in several poetic contests in his native city. Military life also attracted him, and in 1593 he was an officer in the mounted coast guard which had been organized to protect Valencia against raids by Moslem pirates from North Africa.

The dramatist was apparently involved in an unsavory romance with a certain Helena Fenollar some time before his marriage to doña Marquesa Girón de Rebolledo in 1595. His wife died, probably before 1600, but by 1607 at the latest. One of his plays, *Los mal casados de Valencia* (*The Ill-Mated Couples of Valencia*), is a bitter satire on married life, and there are numerous allusions to incompatible couples in others of his plays. There has been some conjecture that these allusions indicate that the dramatist's first marriage was an unhappy one, but there seems to be little or no proof that such was the case.[5]

Sometime after 1602 Castro went to Italy, where in 1607 he was appointed Governor of Scigliano by the Count of Benavente, who was serving as Viceroy of the Kingdom of Naples. Don Guillén was back in Spain in 1609, where he became a member of the expedition which arranged for the transfer from Valencia to North Africa of the Moriscos, Moors who had been converted to Christianity, but who were ordered to leave Spain because they were suspected of religious hypocrisy and of aiding the Moors of North Africa against Spanish interests. The transfer of the banished Valencian Moriscos was completed in November, 1610, after which Castro received permission from his commander, the son of the Viceroy of Naples, to remain in Spain for one year without pay. He was apparently ill between 1610 and 1613, and was unable to return to Italy to resume his duties as Governor of Scigliano, for in 1611 a successor was appointed to that post. But Castro did return to Italy, probably in 1613, where he stayed until the summer of 1616, when he returned to Valencia.

Attempting to revive the tradition of the *Academia de los Nocturnos,* the dramatist founded in 1616 a literary society which he called the *Academia de los montañeses del Parnaso* (*Literary Society of the Dwellers of Mount Parnassus.*) This society, however, lasted only a few months. Castro left Valencia for Madrid, probably in 1618, and success smiled on him in the Spanish capital. He found a powerful patron, don Juan Téllez Girón, son of the famous Duke of Osuna, and took an active part in the literary life of the city. He was invited to join a literary society to which some of the outstanding writers of Spain belonged, among them Lope de Vega, Tirso de Molina, Ruiz de Alarcón, Góngora, Quevedo, and Calderón de la Barca. Castro also took part in several literary contests, in one of which Lope and he were awarded first and second prizes, respectively.

The first plays which our dramatist had published were *El amor constante* (*Constant Love*) and *El caballero bobo* (*The Foolish Young Gentleman*); these were included in a volume of twelve plays by four Valencian dramatists which was published in 1608. His first *Parte* (volume) of twelve plays was published in Valencia in 1618. This volume was reprinted in Valencia in 1621 with a dedication to Marcela, one of the daughters of Lope de Vega. Castro complained that the twelve plays had been reprinted without his permission and that the volume contained numerous errors. But a careful examination of both volumes shows that the 1621 edition was merely a reissue of the 1618 edition. Perhaps Castro used the 1621 edition as an excuse to dedicate it to the daughter of his friend and benefactor, Lope de Vega. There was a close bond between Castro and Lope, evinced by the former's laudatory remarks about Lope in several of his plays. Lope, on the other hand, praised Castro in his *Laurel de Apolo* (*Laurel of Apollo*), and dedicated his play *Las almenas de Toro* (*The Merlons of Toro*) to him.

In 1624 Guillén de Castro was accused of having bribed a well-known criminal to kill a certain nobleman, but an investigation failed to establish his guilt, so the matter was dropped. His second *Parte* of twelve plays was published in Valencia in the following year. This volume was dedicated to his niece, Ana Figueroa y de Castro, and in the explanatory comments to the reader, Castro again complains that during his absence another volume of twelve of his plays had been printed in which there were numerous errors. If such a spurious edition existed, no trace of it has ever come to light.

In 1626 Castro married for the second time, his bride being doña Angela de Salgado, a member of the household of the Duchess of Osuna. Little is known of the last few years of Castro's life. He died in Madrid in 1631 at the age of sixty-two. Many scholars who have delved into his biography have come to the conclusion that he was restless and impulsive, a person who disregarded the usual conventions of society, and one who was utterly incapable of managing his personal financial affairs. There is considerable evidence that during most of his life he suffered from indigence and want, and was constantly in debt. One authority remarks, "for the latter years of his residence in Italy there can be no doubt that dire poverty was the lot of the restless, stubborn and turbulent Don Guillén." [6]

His patron, the Duke of Osuna, deeded a small farm and its income to him in 1619. The dramatist mortgaged this property in 1623, which may well indicate that he needed money to pay his debts. Some scholars go so far as to say that Castro was in such an impoverished condition at his death that he was given a pauper's burial. The assertion seems to have no basis of fact in view of the detailed inventory of his possessions which was made shortly after his death. [7]

II *Castro's Literary Production*

We know that Castro wrote at least twenty-four plays, those which are found in his two *Partes*. Whether he wrote additional plays is a matter for conjecture. Eduardo Juliá Martínez, in his three-volume *Obras de Don Guillén de Castro y Bellvis* includes forty-two three-act plays and a one-act interlude, all of which he considers to have been written by the Valencian playwright. He also includes two plays in which Castro collaborated with other dramatists, several of his poems, three discourses which he delivered to the *Academia de los Nocturnos,* and a careless, anonymous revision of a play which has been attributed to Castro. The question "How many plays did he write?" can be applied to most dramatists of Spain's Golden Age (1550–1681), and in general there is no certain answer. An equally difficult problem is the matter of the composition dates of the plays, a factor of importance for judgments concerning a writer's literary growth and development. Castro's plays, unfortunately, contain very few topical allusions or references to help to establish the dates of composition. Juliá Martínez lists the dramatist's plays in what he considers to be their chronological order. His suggested chronology, which he readily concedes to be hypothetical (Juliá Martínez, *Obras* I, xlvii), is in large measure based on conjecture, and leaves much to be desired.

The late Professor Courtney Bruerton, in an article which deals with the authenticity of the plays ascribed to Guillén de Castro and their chronology, based his work on a careful and systematic study of their versification. In his opinion there are only twenty-seven plays which can with certainty be ascribed to this dramatist: "In this article I accept as definitely authentic only those plays printed by Castro himself in his two *Partes* and *La tragedia por los celos*." [8] In the next few pages, the reader will find Bruerton's list of authentic plays and those of doubtful attribution with his suggested chronological order. A comparison of the chronological order proposed by each of these scholars shows considerable discrepancy. Bruerton, for example, considers *El desengaño dichoso* (*The Happy Revelation*) to be the second play written by the dramatist, and dates it *ca.* 1599. Juliá Martínez proposes the same date (I, lxxxiii), but lists it as Castro's ninth play. Bruerton suggests 1613?–16? for the composition of *Dido y Eneas* (*Dido and Aeneas*). Juliá Martínez states that the versification of the play is suggestive of the author's early technique and gives 1599 as the probable date (II, lxvii). Bruerton's findings indicate that *Cid II* in Juliá Martínez' list was written before *Cid I*.

In addition to the twenty-seven plays which he considers to be authentic, Bruerton believes that three are "Probably by Castro." But he classifies as "Doubtful" or "Texts not by Castro," twelve plays which Juliá Martínez considers to be authentic.

III   *Bruerton's Chronological Tables*

Authentic

El amor constante (*Constant Love*)   1596?–99?
El desengaño dichoso (*The Happy Revelation*)   *ca.* 1599
El nacimiento de Montesinos (*The Birth of Montesinos*)
     1595?–1602?
El conde Alarcos (*Count Alarcos*)   1600?–02
Los mal casados de Valencia (*The Ill-Mated Couples of Valencia*)
     1595?–1604?
El caballero bobo (*The Foolish Young Gentleman*)   1595?–
     1605?
La humildad soberbia (*Proud Humility*)   1595?–1605?

El curioso impertinente (*Dangerous Curiosity*)   1605–08?
    (1605–06?)
Don Quijote de la Mancha (*Don Quijote from la Mancha*)
    1605–08? (1605–06?)
El conde de Irlos (*The Count of Irlos*)   1600?–10? (1605?–08?)
Progne y Filomena (*Procne and Philomela*)   1608?–12?
La verdad averiguada (*Truth Ascertained and the Deceptive
    Marriage*)   1608?–12
La fuerza de la sangre (*Kinship's Powerful Call*)   1613–14
Las mocedades del Cid II (*The Youthful Deeds of the Cid*) (*Cid
    II*)   1610?–15?
El perfecto caballero (*The Perfect Knight*)   1610?–15?
El Narciso en su opinión (*The Self-Styled Narcissus*)   1612?–
    15?
Dido y Eneas (*Dido and Aeneas*)   1613?–16?
Las mocedades del Cid I (*The Youthful Deeds of the Cid*) (*Cid
    I*)   1612?–18? (1612?–15?)
La fuerza de la costumbre (*The Force of Habit*)   1610?–20?
    (1610?–15?)
Los enemigos hermanos (*The Inimical Brothers*)   1615?–20?
    (1615?)
La piedad en la justicia (*Mercy in Justice*)   1615?–20?
    (The title *La justicia en la piedad* is sometimes found.)
El mejor esposo (*The Greatest Spouse*)   1617–20?
La tragedia por los celos (*The Tragedy Caused by Jealousy*)
    1622
El vicio en los extremos (*Vice Carried to Extremes*)   ca. 1623
Cuánto se estima el honor (*How Much One Esteems One's
    Honor*)   1615?–24 (1622?–24)
Engañarse engañando (*The Deceiver Deceived*)   1620?–24
    (1622?–24)
El pretender con pobreza (*The Impoverished Seeker of Royal
    Favor*)   1620?–24

Probably by Castro

Donde no está su dueño . . . (*A Long-Absent Husband Risks
    Dishonor*)   1610?–20?
El ayo de su hijo (*Mentor to His Son*)   1620?–23
Ingratitud por amor (*Ingratitude Caused by Love*)   1620?–28
    (1624?–28)

Doubtful

Las canas en el papel (*A Packet of Gray Hairs and Hesitant Revenge*)

El cerco de Tremecén (*The Siege of Tremecen*)

Las maravillas de Babilonia (*The Marvels of Babylon*)

El nieto de su padre (*His Father's Grandson*)

Pagar en propia moneda (*To Pay One in His Own Coin*)

El pobre honrado (*The Honorable Poor Nobleman*)

Quien no se aventura (*Faint Heart Never Won Fair Lady*)

El renegado arrepentido (*The Repentant Renegade*)

Texts not by Castro

Allá van leyes . . . (*Laws Go where Kings Will*)

Las canas en el papel (Print) (*A Packet of Gray Hairs and Hesitant Revenge*)

El prodigio de los montes . . . (*Santa Barbara, the Prodigy of the Mountains and Martyr of Heaven*)

Quien malas mañas ha . . . (*An Evildoer Repents Late or Never*)[9]

CHAPTER 2

Summaries and Sources

THE comments on sources in this chapter will be limited to certain plays selected from those which Bruerton classifies as "Authentic." These plays are: (1) *Procne and Philomela* and *Dido and Aeneas,* both of which have a Classical background; (2) those plays except *Cid I* and *Cid II* which have been greatly influenced by the rich ballad literature of Spain; (3) *Proud Humility* and *The Tragedy Caused by Jealousy,* which are historical in part, and (4) *Don Quijote from la Mancha, Dangerous Curiosity* and *Kinship's Powerful Call,* which are based on prose works by Cervantes. A summary of *Constant Love* will also be included because it is Castro's first play. Bruerton's chronological order will be followed in each case rather than that suggested by Juliá Martínez. Although the only complete edition of this dramatist's works is the three-volume set edited by Juliá Martínez, the Spanish critic has included other plays which certain scholars do not consider to have been written by the Valencian dramatist, and his chronology, unlike that of Bruerton, is frequently based on what seems to be mere intuition.

I *Constant Love*

The King of Hungary, unhappily married, is in love with Nísida, a lady of the court. But she rebuffs the royal advances, since she is in love with Celauro, the brother of the king, whom the latter has kept imprisoned for fifteen years. Shortly after Celauro's incarceration, Nísida had secretly given birth to a male child, who was then entrusted to the care of a retainer. As the play begins, Celauro is released from prison, but he refuses to accede to the king's request that he give up his love for Nísida. Exiled by the king, Celauro vows that he will return with troops to defeat his brother. The offspring of Celauro and Nísida, whose parents have lost track of him, has been reared as Leonido, the son of a shepherd. Celauro returns to Hungary to attempt to dethrone his brother, but suffering shipwreck and defeat, he unknowingly lives near his beloved Nísida. After defeating Celauro, the king decides to repudiate his queen, after which he will offer to Nísida the choice of marriage to him or death by poison. Encouraged by her father, Nísida chooses poison, and while dying she discloses her secret relations with Celauro, who enters and gives her his hand in marriage. Later, Celauro, mortally wounded by followers of the king, recognizes Leonido as his son by means of a cross which the young man is wearing. Leonido, to avenge his father, kills the tyrannical king, is proclaimed king in his place, and marries a princess whom he had earlier saved from death when she was attacked by a ferocious lion.

Constant Love is Castro's earliest play, and as might be expected, the technique is far from perfect. The author presents a series of loosely-knit incidents rather than a well-developed plot. Most of the characters are violent and unreasoning, and some of their actions are completely incredible, if not silly. Difficult to believe are Leonido's polished courtly speech and manners despite his having been reared as a shepherd's son far removed from the court. The play abounds in melodramatic incidents such as the entrance of a ferocious lion, Celauro's miraculous escape as the only survivor of an immense army, and the recognition of Leonido as Celauro's long-lost son by means of a jeweled cross. The characterization and actions of Nísida stand out in welcome relief against the actions of the other characters and against the melodrama. Castro's handling of the scene in which the king offers her the choice between marriage to him or death by poison is well done, and indicates latent dramatic ability.

Certain subjects and motifs are found in this play which will be dealt with in many of Castro's later plays. A specific instance is his fondness for scenes of violence in which blood is shed. Superstitions of his age are common in Castro's plays, and in *Constant Love* one finds references to such evil omens as the howling of a dog, the breaking of a mirror, and a jewel which for no apparent reason is suddenly propelled from its setting in a ring. Especially reflective of Castro's period are the numerous references to and discussions of the code of honor.

Immediately after the death of his father, Leonido, in a long monologue, vows to refrain from certain pleasures and comforts until he has killed his father's enemy. The tone of this monologue is reminiscent of the famous ballad *Fonte-frida, Fonte-frida*, in which the turtledove, whose mate has died, seeks sorrow and discomfort rather than solace and pleasure. This is especially true of Leonido's specific vow "not to look for water and not to drink it without first making its beautiful clearness turbid" (Juliá M., I, 43b). The corresponding line in the ballad is "for if I find the water clear—I drink it turbid." Thus we find Castro's interest in the ballads of Spain making itself evident in his first play. One line in the play, *con inmortales pies pisas y mides* (I, 39a) is taken in its entirety from the next-to-last stanza of Garcilaso de la Vega's *Egloga primera*.

II   *The Birth of Montesinos*

Castro's use of ballad material in *Constant Love* is merely incidental, but in *The Birth of Montesinos* we have a play that is based on two rather long minstrel or juglaresque ballads, from which the dramatist quotes several passages almost word for word. Montesinos, as students of Spanish balladry recall, is the hero of several minstrel ballads, the best known being the one in which he promises his friend Durandarte, who was mortally wounded in the battle of Roncesvalles, to carry his heart to his fiancée, Belerma. Cervantes based the episode of *The Cave of Montesinos* in Part Two of *The Quijote* upon this ballad.

The first of the ballad sources for the Castro play is number 382 in Durán's collection, which begins, *Muchas veces oí decir / y a los antiguos contar* ("Many times have I heard it said / and heard old people relate").[1] In this ballad, Grimaltos, at the court of Charlemagne, rises from the position of page to the ranks of chamberlain, secretary, and then governor. After his marriage to the king's daughter, he and his wife leave for his domain in Leon, where he rules wisely and justly. Five years pass. Don Tomillas, a treacherous member of Charlemagne's court, persuades the king that Grimaltos is planning to rebel against him. The king decides to have Grimaltos put to death. Meanwhile, Grimaltos has a prophetic dream which leads him to believe that evil days are in store for him. He and his wife return to Paris, where the king upbraids him and orders him to leave the kingdom within three days. His wife, pregnant, leaves with him.

The two wander through the wilderness for three days, suffering from hunger and fatigue, when a son is born to them. A kind hermit provides food and shelter, and baptizes the child with the name Montesinos, since he was born in the mountains. Grimaltos and his family stay in the neighborhood for fifteen years as the father trains his son as a knight should be trained, to handle weapons, to hunt, to read and write, and to play backgammon. One St. John's Day, when Grimaltos and Montesinos see Paris from a lofty peak, the father, affected by tears and sobs, talks to his son.

Castro's second ballad source begins, *Cata Francia, Montesinos, / cata París la ciudad* ("Behold France, Montesinos, / behold the city of Paris").[2] After Grimaltos tells his son of the treachery committed by don Tomillas, Montesinos goes to Paris in order to avenge his father. As he watches the king and don Tomillas play chess, Montesinos calls attention to the fact that don Tomillas is cheating. A fight ensues in which Montesinos kills the villain. He then gives the king an account of the many misdeeds committed by don Tomillas. The king summons Grimaltos and his wife to Paris, where they are royally received and their former possessions are restored to them.

In his version of this ballad, Castro makes use of his prerogative to embellish and to deviate to a certain extent from his sources. Quite foreign to the ballad is Isabella, with her amorous interest in Grimaltos, her subsequent marriage to Charlemagne, and her false story of being pregnant. In the play the princess gives birth, not to one child as in the ballad, but to twins, one of whom Isabella passes off as her own. In the ballad, Montesinos kills don Tomillas, while in the play he merely wounds him. The dramatist has gone directly to the two ballads for specific details and includes in the play lines which are taken either directly from his sources or lines which are revised very slightly because of the substitution of other verse forms for the typical ballad assonance.

III *Count Alarcos*

Castro's next play in Bruerton's list is also based on a long minstrel ballad, *Retraída está la infanta, / bien así como solía* ("The princess is in seclusion, as she was wont to be").[3] The princess, unhappy because she is not married, tells her father, the king, that Count Alarcos had promised to become her husband, a promise which he broke when he married another. The king, convinced that his daughter is telling the truth, orders the count to kill his wife and then marry the princess. The count carries out the order by strangling his wife with her headdress. Before she dies, she forgives him, but she summons the king and princess to appear soon before God's seat of judgment. The count, the king, and the princess die before the lapse of thirty days. The ballad reflects the belief in the efficacy of a victim's summoning those who have wronged him to appear before the seat of divine judgment (the summoning on a certain date was called *el emplazamiento*), a belief which was widely held during the Middle Ages.

In the play, Margarita, the fiancée of Count Alarcos, gives secret birth to their son. The jealous princess takes the child from Margarita, hoping to use the infant to win the affections of the count. But she fails to do so, and the count marries Margarita. For revenge, the princess orders Hortensio, a servant, to kill Carlos, the son of Alarcos and Margarita, after which he must serve the child's heart and blood to its parents, who are to be unaware of what food is being served to them. Later, a daughter, Elena, is born to the count and Margarita. The persistent princess convinces her father that the count had seduced her. The king thereupon orders Alarcos to kill his wife and marry the princess. Forced to obey the cruel mandate, the count throttles his wife and leaves her for dead. But her life is saved by Hortensio, who had fled the court. Alarcos, dressed in mourning, marries the princess.

Margarita and Hortensio live in the wilderness as savages along with Carlos, the son of Alarcos and Margarita. Through a series of melodramatic circumstances, all the main characters meet near Hortensio's cave. The latter explains that, instead of killing Carlos and serving his heart and blood to his parents, he had really served them the flesh and blood of a lamb. The princess confesses her guilt, promising to retire to a convent. All other difficulties are resolved. The king and Alarcos are reconciled as the latter and Margarita are joyfully reunited.

IV *Proud Humility*

The protagonist, don Rodrigo de Villandrando, is a historical character, but the work itself cannot be called a genuinely historical play. Rodrigo's proud father, don Juan, persuades him not to marry the rich and powerful doña María de Zúñiga although the Villandrando fortunes are at a low ebb. Even though María compromises her honor by coming to his home, Rodrigo refuses to marry her and goes to France to seek his fortune. There he helps the French in their war against the English. He saves the French king from being captured, and is greatly honored for his deeds, eventually marrying Margarita, the niece of the French king. Later Rodrigo loses favor with the king, but after he kills the English champion Talabote (Talbot), he is restored to favor. Word comes to Rodrigo that his father has been imprisoned and will be executed shortly unless Rodrigo returns to Spain to marry María, who claims that he had seduced her. Rodrigo, powerful and wealthy, accompanied by his wife, returns to Spain where he secures the release of his father. María and Margarita quarrel over Rodrigo, and in a confused melee Rodrigo unwittingly mortally wounds Margarita by hurling his dagger. At the king's behest, Rodrigo marries María.

The life of the legendary don Rodrigo de Villandrando and Count of Ribadeo is dealt with in a chronicle published in 1486, in which one finds the following reference to his possessions: ". . . and he was lord of twenty-seven towns in Bourbon territory, some of which he bought and some of which he won." [4] A paraphrase of this statement by Rodrigo in the play indicates Castro's acquaintance with Pulgar's *Chronicle*: "All told, I have in Bourgogne twenty-seven good towns, some of which were bought, and some of which were won in fine warfare" (I, 488b).

In Pulgar's account, young Rodrigo goes to France where he takes service under a French captain, and soon earns an outstanding reputation as a soldier. Losing favor with his commander because of jealousy and hatred aroused by his success, he and a few friends form a mercenary band which Rodrigo leads in frequent raids against the English. After he acquires considerable wealth, Rodrigo marries Margarita, daughter of the Duke of Bourbon. The English champion, Talabote,[5] invites him to have food and drink, after which the two armies will engage in battle, but Rodrigo refuses the invitation. He returns to Spain, where he marries Beatriz de Stúñiga (and not María de Zúñiga) after the death of his French wife.

Many of Rodrigo's acts of derring-do in the play, such as his killing of Talabote on the field of battle, his rescue of the King of France, and his capture of the King of England, have no basis in fact. The third act especially shows numerous deviations from

Pulgar's *Chronicle*, one of the most notable of which is the accidental fatal wounding of Margarita.

V *Dangerous Curiosity*

Cervantes' *Don Quijote de la Mancha* has been the inspiration for several Spanish plays. Guillén de Castro based two of his dramas, *Dangerous Curiosity* and *Don Quijote from la Mancha*, on the first part of the novel, which was published in 1605. Bruerton ascribes the dates of 1605–08? (1605–06?) to each of these plays, which suggests that Castro wasted little if any time in bringing these two episodes from the novel to the stage. *Dangerous Curiosity* ("El curioso impertinente" in the *Quijote*) is the dramatization of Chapters 33–35 of Cervantes' work. In the latter's version, two young men of Florence, Lotario and Anselmo, are bosom friends. Anselmo marries Camila, a beautiful and virtuous young lady, but shortly after, he is assailed by a morbid doubt: is Camila as good and perfect as she seems to be, and could her virtue be undermined by a rival for her affections? Anselmo asks Lotario to test her virtue, but his friend indignantly refuses to do so. Only when Anselmo vows to have some other man undertake the task does Lotario yield to the pleas of his friend. Lotario gradually falls in love with Camila during Anselmo's contrived absences from home, and Camila gradually becomes interested in him, with the result that she finally yields to him. When Anselmo learns of his wife's infidelity, he dies of sorrow. Lotario becomes a soldier and is killed in battle. Camila becomes a nun, but she too soon dies of sorrow.

In Castro's adaptation, when Anselmo discovers his wife and friend in a lovers' tryst, a duel ensues in which Anselmo is mortally wounded. Before he dies, he acknowledges that he alone is to blame for the tragedy, he forgives Lotario and decrees that Camila and her lover should gain possession of all his property after they are married. In the play, many characters are included who are not found in the novel, among them the duke, the duchess, Culebro, and Torcato. Where Cervantes has limited himself to one plot, Castro has two subplots. In one instance, at least, Castro quotes directly from the novel in parts of a veiled letter which Camila writes to Anselmo, in which she informs him that unless he soon returns home, she will go to live with her parents during his absence.[6]

VI   *Don Quijote de la Mancha*

This play is based on Chapters 23–36 of *Part One* of Cervantes' novel. In the prose version, Cardenio, of noble parentage, is in love with Luscinda. Overcome with grief when he is deceived into believing that Luscinda will marry Fernando, a false friend of his, Cardenio flees to Sierra Morena where he lives the life of a savage. Dorotea, a victim of Fernando's false promises, also comes to Sierra Morena, where in disguise she serves as a shepherd. A barber and a priest, who have come to Sierra Morena in search of their friend, don Quijote, use Dorotea as a lure in order to persuade don Quijote to return home. The group, composed of don Quijote, Sancho, Cardenio, Dorotea, the priest and the barber, stops at an inn where the priest reads to his companions the story *Dangerous Curiosity*. Fernando and the heartbroken Luscinda happen to stop at this inn with the result that Fernando, after fervent pleas from the other guests, promises to accept Dorotea as his wife, which leaves Cardenio and Luscinda free to marry.

Castro's play follows the general theme of the tale by Cervantes. Cardenio, son of a peasant, and Lucinda, a young lady of noble parentage, are very much in love. A young marquis, with whom Cardenio has been raised, is a cowardly despicable person who has earned the contempt of all, including his father, a duke. The marquis, after seducing and abandoning Dorotea, the daughter of a shepherd, centers his attention upon Lucinda. Ordered by her father to marry the marquis, Lucinda flees from home just before the ceremony is to begin. Cardenio, believing that Lucinda has married the marquis, loses his reason and seeks refuge in the wilderness where don Quijote, who had previously tried to help Dorotea and Lucinda, is doing self-imposed penance. The priest and the barber make use of Dorotea to lure don Quijote away. As the play ends, the cowardly marquis turns out to be the son of a peasant whose mother had substituted him at birth for Cardenio, the real son of the duke. Cardenio and Lucinda marry, as do Dorotea and the false marquis, who has been forgiven for his misdeeds. Don Quijote goes home in a cage.

The modern reader, to whom don Quijote is a lofty, noble figure who has charmed and captivated people of many generations, will be greatly disappointed in Castro's depiction of him. The dramatist presents Cervantes' great hero as a crude, ridicu-

lous, pitiful caricature bereft of reason. One incident in the play
will be taken as typical of Castro's presentation. When Luscinda
writes to Cardenio asking him to come to her aid, she promises to
leave a light burning in her window as a signal. Don Quijote,
seeing this light, is under the delusion that Ero (Hero) is summoning him to swim the Hellespont. So he removes some of his
clothes and crudely makes his way across the stage as if he were
swimming, much to the discomfiture of Sancho.[7]

VII *Count Irlos*

The long ballad, *Estábase el conde Dirlos,* / *sobrino de don
Beltrane,* / *asentado en las sus tierras,* / *deleitándose en cazare*
("Count Dirlos, the nephew of don Beltrán, was settled on his
lands, enjoying the pleasures of the chase"),[8] deals with the life of
this peer of Charlemagne's court. The count's happy life is interrupted when he receives a letter from his uncle Charlemagne, re-
questing that he lead an expedition against King Aliarde. Leaving
his wife in Paris in the care of his uncle, Irlos embarks with his
men for Persia. He conquers the territory held by Aliarde, but
stays on in Persia for fifteen years without sending any word
home, which leads many people in France to believe that he has
died. The count, who has let his hair and beard grow, has a dream
in which he sees his wife in the arms of Prince Celinos. When he
awakens he tells his men that it is time for them to return to
France, but he admonishes them not to disclose his identity. Back
in his homeland, he learns that his former possessions are now
owned by Prince Celinos, who has spread false reports that Irlos
has died. Countess Irlos has been forced to marry Celinos, but
only with the proviso that the marriage will not be consummated.
The count secretly goes to Paris where he discloses his identity
and accuses some of the peers of not protecting his interests during his absence. Violent words ensue, civil war threatens the nation, but peace is finally restored when Charlemagne promises to
impose certain restraints on Celinos. The count then cuts his hair
and beard, and his former estates are restored to him.

In the play, Castro improvises to a great extent. Several of his
characters are not found in the ballad, among them Melisendra,
Leonora, Rocandolfo, and Malgesí. Irlos is chosen by lot to lead
the expedition against Aliarde, and this, contrary to the ballad,

happens before he marries the countess. In fact, practically all of the first act is extraneous to the ballad. In the play, the absence of Irlos from France lasts for ten years, three months, and two days instead of the fifteen years in the ballad. A great deal of the third act is improvisation. The play has several scenes of magic which are not wholly convincing, and which must have strained the crude stage devices of Castro's time. Typical are the scenes in which the count sees Celinos throw Marfira's head to the stage after he decapitates her, and where the earth opens and swallows Landín. The latter is one of the dramatist's earliest comic characters, and his introduction shows that Castro is beginning to give attention to humorous aspects in his plays.

VIII *Procne and Philomela*

There are numerous versions of the tragic story of these two sisters, the best known of which is undoubtedly Ovid's in Book VI of his *Metamorphoses*. In this version, Tereus, King of Thrace, marries Procne (Progne in Castro's play), daughter of King Pandion of Athens. Baleful omens at the wedding are strongly suggestive of the tragic events which are to follow. Tereus takes his bride to Thrace, where a son Itys is born to them. Five years pass; Procne, longing to see her sister, Philomela (Castro's Filomena), asks her husband either to let her return to Athens for a short visit or to bring her sister to her. Tereus goes to Athens in order to bring Philomela to Thrace. But when he sees Procne's beautiful sister, he falls violently in love with her and makes up his mind to seduce her. He escorts her to Thrace, but as soon as they land he drags her into the deep woods and forces her into a decrepit hut where he rapes her. When she vows to proclaim publicly the vile deed, he cuts off her tongue. Leaving her confined in the hut, he goes home where he tells Procne that her sister is dead.

A year goes by. Philomela, unable to talk or flee, weaves the story of her attack on a cloth which she manages to have delivered to her sister, who releases her from the hut and takes her to the palace. Seeing her son Itys, Procne remarks to herself: "How like his father he is!" and driven by an overpowering desire to avenge her sister, she kills the child. Procne and Philomela then cut up the body and cook part of it, which they serve to the unsuspecting Tereus. When he asks for his son, Philomela, covered with blood,

enters and hurls the bloody head of his son at him. Tereus, drawing his sword, pursues the two sisters whom the gods save by
changing them into birds with blood-red feathers. Tereus is punished by being changed into a hoopoe, an ugly bird which is un-
clean in both its food and in its habits.

Numerous details in the play show that Castro was well acquainted with the myth. The names of four of his main characters
are Progne, Filomena, Tereo, and Itis. Filomena is attacked by
Tereo, who slashes her tongue. She informs her sister of the attack
by means of a woven cloth. Progne kills her son, cooks and serves
his heart to Tereo. But the exigencies of stagecraft dictated numerous changes and the addition of extraneous elements. Thus,
Tereo is kept from marrying Filomena, whom he wanted for his
bride, and becomes the unwilling husband of Progne because of
an error in the labeling of portraits of the two sisters. Teosindo,
the brother of Tereo and fiancé of Filomena, is a new character.
Tereo and Progne have two children instead of the one in the
mythic version. Filomena, who disappears after she is attacked by
Tereo, vows never to speak again and retires to the wilderness
where, with her son Driante, she lives as a savage in a lonely cave
(a favorite theme of the dramatist). Also completely extraneous
to the myth is the civil war, because of which Progne takes refuge
in Filomena's cave, where she recognizes her sister. When Tereo
and Teosindo appear on the scene, Filomena breaks her vow of
perpetual silence in order to save Teosindo's life. The various
members of the two families are thus reunited and all is forgiven.
Castro, with his fondness for bringing scenes of bloodshed to the
stage, must have felt a close kinship with the author of the myth
of Procne and Philomela as it has come down in Ovid's *Metamorphoses*.

In his chronology Juliá Martínez lists this as the fourth play by
Castro. But *Procne and Philomela* is vastly superior to *Constant
Love* and *The Foolish Young Gentleman* in characterization, plot,
and poetic expression, which would seem to indicate that Castro
has developed considerably in mastering dramatic technique. This
does not mean that the work has no major defects, for much of the
third act is for the modern reader highly melodramatic and improbable. The characterization of Driante and Arminda leaves
much to be desired. But the superiority of this play over the two

which are mentioned immediately above is so great that one can
ask with reason whether Juliá Martínez is justified in placing it so
early in the dramatist's career. Bruerton's suggestion that it is Castro's eleventh play and his dates 1608?–12? seem quite acceptable.

IX *Kinship's Powerful Call*

Cervantes published his collection of *Novelas Ejemplares* (*Exemplary Tales*) in 1613. One of these tales, *La fuerza de la sangre*,
is the source of Castro's play of the same name. In Cervantes'
story, a young libertine Rodolfo abducts a young lady named
Leocadia. He takes her to his home where he ravishes her while
she is unconscious. Leocadia, on regaining consciousness, makes a
mental inventory of the room and takes a silver crucifix with her
when she is released. Luis, the son born to her as the result of the
attack, is reared for a few years in a small town before he is
brought to her home where he is passed off as her nephew. While
he is out on the street one day, Luis is trampled and severely
injured by a horse. An elderly gentleman who witnesses the acci-
dent is irresistibly drawn by a powerful force toward the youngster, who reminds him in some way of his son Rodolfo. Leocadia,
informed of what has happened to her son, hurries to the home of
the elderly gentleman, where she recognizes the room in which
she had lost her honor. Her story and the silver crucifix which she
later shows them convince Rodolfo's parents that their son is
the child's father. They summon Rodolfo home where the mother
contrives to have him meet Leocadia. Attracted by her beauty, he
gladly consents to marry her at once when he learns that she is the
young lady whom he had violated.

Guillén de Castro complicates the plot and adds dramatic interest by having two female victims abducted instead of the one in
the version by Cervantes. The victims are Lidora and her cousin
Isbella, who are abducted and raped by Grisanto and Rodulfo,
respectively. Lidora gives birth to a son, who, as in the Cervantine
tale, is trampled by a horse in the presence of Honorio, the father
of Grisanto. Honorio, attracted by the child, takes him home with
him. Lidora hurries to the side of her son and recognizes the room
in which she had been the victim of Grisanto's lust. Isbella also
goes to the home of Honorio, where she likewise recognizes the
room in which she had been attacked. Each young lady feels cer-

tain that Grisanto was the one responsible for the loss of her honor. When Lidora produces the crucifix which she had taken from Grisanto's room, he accepts that as sufficient proof and marries her. Rodulfo then takes Isbella for his wife. The reader will note that Castro has made certain changes in the names of Cervantes' characters.

X Dido and Aeneas

The first four books of Virgil's *Aeneid* are the source of the greater part of Castro's *Dido and Aeneas*. Insofar as events are concerned, the dramatist follows Virgil's epic quite closely so that John Dryden's arguments of the first four books of his translation of the Latin poem give the reader an excellent idea of what is to be found in the play. Dryden tells how the Trojans, after the fall of Troy, set sail for Italy. Driven to an African port by a storm, Aeneas meets his mother, Venus, who appears in the shape of a huntress. She conveys him to Carthage where he meets companions whom he had believed to be lost in the storm. Queen Dido of Carthage, as the result of a device of Venus, begins to have a passion for him. Here there is a flashback as Aeneas gives Dido an account of the fall of Troy. As the story resumes, Dido, who has thoughts of marrying Aeneas, prepares a hunting party for his entertainment. A storm drives the two of them into a cave, where passion prevails. Mercury soon warns Aeneas to leave Carthage. Dido tries to keep him from leaving, but not being able to persuade him to stay with her, she contrives her own death.

The opening scenes of the play deal with the fall of Troy and the ensuing slaughter of many of its citizens. In addition to this deviation in chronology from the epic poem, a few minor episodes in the play are not found in Virgil's poem. One such episode is the execution of Celeusia for violating Dido's mandate that widows should not remarry (I, 178b ff.). Another is the meeting of Aeneas and Hiarbas in Carthage after Dido has killed herself with the sword of Aeneas. Castro makes use of two ballads for secondary source material in this play. Shortly after the arrival of Aeneas in Carthage, Dido invites him to dine with her. After dinner she asks him to continue his interrupted account of the destruction of Troy. The first few lines of this scene and the first few lines of a well-known ballad are given below. Castro's indebtedness to the ballad is quite evident:

Castro	Ballad
After dinner the devout Trojan wishes to tell the widow of Sychaeous and foundress of Carthage about the sad holocaust of Troy. (*Contar quiere sobre mesa el piadoso troyano a la viuda de Siqueo, fundadora de Cartago, de Troya el incendio triste, . . .*) (I, 180b)	After dinner the devout Trojan tells the widow of Sychaeous and foundress of Carthage how the famous city of Troy was a field of ashes because of that lifeless horse filled with live Greeks. (*Contando está sobre-mesa el piadoso troyano a la viuda de Siqueo, fundadora de Cartago, como la famosa Troya era de cenizas campo por aquel caballo muerto, de vivos griegos preñado.*)[9]

The other ballad which serves as a secondary source begins:

> Through the woods of Carthage Queen Dido and Aeneas went out a-hunting accompanied by many riders.
> (*Por los bosques de Cartago salían a montería la reina Dido y Eneas con muy gran caballería.*)[10]

While this ballad provides Castro with a few details not found in Virgil's account of the hunting party, the dramatist does not quote any of its lines directly. But a comparison of the two versions shows that the dramatist is again indebted to a ballad. The characterization in this play is well done, and there are some highly effective dramatic scenes, especially in the third act, between Dido and Aeneas. The introduction of the supernatural elements does not detract greatly from this play that is on the whole well written and enjoyable.

XI *The Tragedy Caused by Jealousy*

King Alfonso of Aragon and doña Margarita have been lovers for several years and a son, Fernando, has been born to them. The king has every hope of eventual marriage to Margarita, but affairs of state force him to marry the dour and vindictive Princess María. María, aware of Alfonso's interest in Margarita, has become jealous of her, and warns her that if she shows herself receptive to any advances from the king she will kill her. About a year after his marriage to María, the king tries to renew his relations with Margarita. When the queen learns of this, she warns Margarita for the second time. The king persists, however, and promises Margarita that if she yields to his pleas she will be allowed to see her son Fernando, who has been reared away from the palace. Margarita sends a message to the king in which she informs him that he may call on her that evening. Shortly after he receives the message, Alfonso sees a hawk kill a white dove and he overhears a peasant sing a sad ballad about the violent death of Inés de Castro, the beautiful wife of Prince Pedro of Portugal, who was murdered in 1335 by jealous courtiers. These apparently evil omens arouse a feeling of apprehension in Alfonso, who hurriedly rides home to Margarita, only to find that she has been cruelly murdered by María. Alfonso, after informing the queen that he will never see her again, takes his son with him to Naples.

Castro's play is in large part historical. Alfonso V, King of Aragon and Catalonia, married his cousin doña María of Castile in 1415, but their marriage was without issue. The King neglected his wife and became interested in Margarita de Híjar, who, according to some accounts, was the mother of his illegitimate son Fernando. It is generally agreed that María murdered Margarita because of her belief that Margarita was the mother of Fernando. Alfonso never forgave the Queen and departed for Italy with his son. María, who never again saw her husband, served as regent of Aragon until her death. Her unhappy life is narrated in the ballad, *Retraída estaba la reina*, / *la muy casta doña María* ("The queen was in seclusion, the most chaste doña María").[11] Two other characters in the play, Vique and Corella, are historical. It is interesting to note that the love affair of Alfonso with Margarita has much in common with the legend of Inés de Castro.

The dramatist's interest in the rich balladry of Spain is again evident in this play. The ill-omened song which Alfonso hears as he is about to leave for his tryst with Margarita is based on one of the many variants of the ballad *El palmero* (*The Palmer*). In the first part of this ballad a young man in high spirits is on his way from Valladolid to Burgos, ostensibly to see his beloved. He meets a palmer who informs him that his beloved has just suffered death as the result of numerous thrusts from a dagger.

CHAPTER 3

Castro's Versification and the Dating of his Plays

S PANISH poets and dramatists of the Golden Age had at their
disposal various nationally originated verse forms in addition
to several which had developed in Italy during the Renaissance.
Guillén de Castro makes abundant use of four of these Spanish
strophes: *redondillas, quintillas, décimas,* and *versos de romance.*
Another national type, assonants of seven syllables called *roman-
cillos,* appears in only one of his plays.

The *redondilla* is a stanza of four octosyllabic lines which
rhyme *abba.* That is, lines one and four rhyme, as do lines two
and three. There is a prosodic stress on the seventh syllable of
each line, which is a characteristic of Spanish octosyllabic verses.
In the following *redondilla,* introduced here to demonstrate this
strophe, the Cid's father explains to the king how he had washed
away his dishonor with the blood of his enemy after the Cid had
killed Count Lozano:

> *Lavé con sangre el lugar*
> *adonde la mancha estaba,*
> *porque el honor que se lava,*
> *con sangre se ha de lavar.* (II, 182a)

(With blood I washed the place where my honor had been
stained, because honor which is washed clean must be washed
with blood.)

In scanning Spanish poetry, a syllable following the last
stressed syllable is always counted, whether or not the line actu-
ally contains such a syllable. Thus in the *redondilla* given above,
lines two and three have eight syllables by actual count. (Observe
that in line two *-cha es-* of *mancha estaba* blend to form one syllable. In line three *-que el* of *porque el* combine to form one syllable. This blending or combining into one syllable of two or more

contiguous vowels of separate words is called "synalepha.") But lines one and four which end in a stressed seventh syllable are still considered to be octosyllabic.

The *quintilla* is a strophe of five octosyllabic lines with two rhymes, and not more than two consecutive lines should have the same rhyme. There are five common types of *quintilla,* which rhyme as follows: (1), *ababa;* (2), *abbab;* (3), *abaab;* (4), *aabab;* (5), *aabba.*[1] In the following *quintilla,* which is type 1, King Fernando suggests to his son Sancho that he is still quite young to wield a sword:

REY.	Pareceráte pesada,
	que tus años tiernos son.
DON SANCHO.	Ya desnuda o ya envainada,
	las alas del corazón
	hacen ligera la espada. (II, 170b)

(KING. It will seem heavy to you because of your tender years. DON SANCHO. Whether the sword is drawn or sheathed, the wings of my heart make it seem light.)

The *décima* consists of ten octosyllabic verses, which rhyme *abbaaccddc.* The perfect *décima* has a definite pause at the end of line four. This poetic form is sometimes called *espinela,* because of the belief once held that the Spanish writer Vicente Espinel had been its creator. In the following *décima,* Diego Laínez, after he has been dishonored by Count Lozano, breaks his staff in two and then soliloquizes on his action:

> ¡Cielos! ¡Peno, muero, rabio! . . .
> No más báculo rompido,
> pues sustentar no ha podido,
> sino al honor, al agravio.
> Mas no os culpo, como sabio;
> mal he dicho . . . perdonad:
> que es ligera autoridad
> la vuestra, y sólo sustenta,
> no la carga de una afrenta,
> sino el peso de una edad.   (II, 174b)

(Heavens! How I suffer, die and rage! No longer do I want this broken staff, since it has not been able to uphold my honor nor to bear the affront. But wisely I do not blame you; I am wrong . . . forgive me. For a light responsibility is yours since it must support only the weight of old age and not the burden of an affront.)

The *verso de romance,* or ballad meter, is the most thoroughly national of all Spanish meters, and was a popular form with the dramatists and poets of the Golden Age. It has maintained its popularity down to the present day. The lines are octosyllabic, and the even-numbered lines, instead of having consonantal rhyme, have a single assonance throughout the passage, which may vary in length from a few lines to several pages. In assonance there is identity of the last stressed vowel and any following vowel or vowels in the even-numbered lines, while at the same time there is complete disregard of any consonant which follows the last stressed vowel. Thus in the words *mandas, alma, canta,* there is assonance in *a-a; años, Lozano, contralto* have assonance in *a-o,* while *mira, vista, divisan* have assonance in *i-a.* Examples of assonance in English can be found in proverbs, nursery rhymes, and cowboy ballads. Typical are "Little Tommy Tucker sings for his supper" and "See a pin and pick it up and all the day you'll have good luck," where there is assonance in *u-e* and *u,* respectively.

A well-known passage of *verso de romance* by Guillén de Castro is found in *Cid II,* when Arias Gonzalo, from the walls of Zamora, shouts a warning to King Sancho to beware of the treacherous Bellido de Olfos:

> ARIAS. . . . *que de Zamora ha salido,*
> *Bellido de Olfos llamado,*
> *traidor, hijo de traidores.*
> *El hechizo de sus labios*
> *no te engañe, que a su padre*
> *y a su misma sangre ingrato,*
> *le mató y echó en un río;*
> *testigo bien declarado*
> *de quien es. Matarte quiere;*
> *toma mi consejo llano.*
> *No digas que no te aviso;*
> *no acuerdes tarde, don Sancho.*   (II, 222a)

(ARIAS. . . . For there has gone forth from Zamora one who is named Bellido de Olfos, a traitor, son of traitors. Let not the wicked spell of his lips deceive you, because he, ungrateful to his father and his own blood, killed him and cast him in a stream, which is well-declared evidence of what he is. He wants to kill you. Accept my unvarnished advice. Do not say that I have not warned you. Don't remember too late, don Sancho.)

During the fifteenth and sixteenth centuries, Renaissance Italy was supreme in intellectual matters as well as in most other manifestations of civilization. Her many brilliant writers were imitated throughout Western Europe, and the interpretations of Aristotle and Horace by her literary critics received general and unquestioned acceptation. So it is not surprising to find that Italian poetic forms were eventually taken over by Spanish poets. The first attempt to acclimatize an Italian strophe in Spain was made by the first Marquis of Santillana, Iñigo López de Mendoza (1398–1458), who wrote forty-two sonnets, in many of which one can find direct imitations of the Italian poet Petrarch. But whether the efforts of López de Mendoza came too early, or whether he lacked the requisite poetic temperament to master the new style, it was not until 1526 that Italian poetic forms received complete and permanent acceptance in Spanish poetry.

In that year Andrea Navagero, the ambassador from Venice, suggested to the Spanish poet Juan Boscán that he employ Italian meters in writing poetry, since the Italian meters were superior to those of Spain. Boscán accepted the suggestion, and produced poetry in which he followed Italian models. Thanks to Boscán, and especially to his gifted friend Garcilaso de la Vega, strophes of the Italian Renaissance have formed an integral part of Spanish poetry since that time. Seven of these Italian poetic forms are found in the plays of Guillén de Castro in addition to the four Spanish strophes used extensively by him. These will be discussed in the order in which they are dealt with by Bruerton in his article "The Chronology of the *Comedias* of Guillén de Castro." [2]

Silva. This is a passage of indefinite length with lines of eleven or of eleven and seven syllables. Most of the lines rhyme, but there is usually no fixed order of rhyme. Four types of *silva* have been distinguished, called *silva 1°, 2°, 3°,* and *4°.*[3] Type 2° is the only one found in the plays which Bruerton considers to be authentic Castro. This type, which consists of lines of seven and eleven syllables mixed irregularly with no fixed order of rhyme, and in which some unrhymed lines may be found, is exemplified by the following passage from *Vice Carried to Extremes:*

ALVARO. *¿Dónde estoy? ¿Qué mudanza*
           he visto en mi cuidado?
           ¿Qué hielo en mi esperanza?
           ¿Con qué monte he topado?
           ¿Qué nubes han pasado
           por mis ojos? ¿Qué fuego
           me tuvo mudo y me detiene ciego?
           ¿Qué confusión me espanta?
           ¿Qué nudo se me ha puesto en la garganta?
           ¿Con qué lazo me ahoga?
           ¿A qué suplicio voy, que aun no me deja
           mover los pies para arrastrar la soga?   (III, 348a)

(ALVARO. Where am I? What change have I seen in my love affair? What lack of warmth in my hopes? What mountain have I come up against? What clouds have passed before my eyes? What fire held me mute and blindly stops me? What confusion frightens me? What knot has been placed around my neck? With what cord does it stifle me? To what torment do I go which does not even let me move my feet in order to drag the halter?)

In the eleven-syllable (hendecasyllabic) verse, there is an obligatory stress on the tenth syllable, and other stresses will generally, but not always, be found on the fourth or sixth or eighth syllables, either singly or in combination. Thus in the first line of eleven syllables quoted above, *me tuvo mudo y me detiene ciego* there are major stresses on the fourth, eighth and tenth syllables, while in the next line of eleven syllables *¿Qué nudo se me ha puesto en la garganta?* there are major stresses on the sixth and tenth syllables. In the shorter lines of seven syllables, called heptasyllabic, there is an obligatory stress on the sixth syllable.

Octava Real. This strophe, which was not highly favored by Guillén de Castro, consists of eight lines of eleven syllables, with the rhyme ABABABCC. (It should be noted that the capital letters are used to indicate hendecasyllables, and small letters will indicate lines of eight or fewer syllables.) The following *octava real* is an apostrophe to the inflexible code of honor by a father who believes that he has killed his daughter in order to prevent the violation of her honor:

           ¡Ay, santo honor; qué bien te llama santo
           quien tus milagros valeroso advierte!

> *¡Cuánto debe estimarte, cuánto, cuánto,*
> *quien llega, por tratarte, a conocerte!*
> *¡Tanto te estimo yo, a quien cuestas tanto,*
> *que con dar sentimientos a la muerte*
> *de Cecilia, tan de padre, no he podido*
> *estar de habella muerto arrepentido!*   (II, 119b)

(Alas, sanctified honor; how well does one who bravely bears in mind your miracles call you sanctified! How greatly must one who comes to know you at first hand hold you in esteem! You are held in high esteem by me to whom your burden is so costly, that despite my fatherly grief over Cecilia's death, I have not been able to feel repentant over having killed her.)

Sonnet. Spanish poets gave preference to the Italian or Petrarchan sonnet with its two quatrains of eleven-syllable lines rhyming *ABBA ABBA* followed by two tercets or a sextet with various rhymes such as *CDCDCD, CDECDE,* etc. This strophe is not common in authentic Castro, there being a total of seven in four plays. The following sonnet is found in *The Self-Styled Narcissus:*

> *Apenas tiene pluma el avecilla,*
> *cuando pone en los vientos el cuidado:*
> *el más menudo pez del mar salado*
> *suele atreverse a su arenosa orilla.*
> *Deja el monte la tierna cervatilla,*
> *y aunque con su peligro pace el prado,*
> *las útiles defensas de ganado*
> *pierde tal vez la mansa corderilla.*
> *Sube al aire la tierra más pesada,*
> *sale de madre el más pequeño río,*
> *el cobarde mayor saca la espada;*
> *la menor esperanza finge brío,*
> *¡y solamente la mujer honrada*
> *tiene sin libertad el albedrío!*   (III, 90a)

(No sooner does the tiny bird have feathers than it puts its cares into the wind; the smallest fish in the briny sea often dares to test its sandy shore. The tender little deer leaves the forest, and although in peril it grazes in the meadow, the gentle lamb loses perhaps the useful defenses common to a flock. The heaviest bit of earth goes sailing skyward, the smallest river overflows its banks, the most abject of cowards unsheathes his sword, the slightest bit of hope feigns courage, and only does the woman who has honor find her free will unfree!)

Tercetos. This strophe consists of hendecasyllables which rhyme *ABA BCB CDC*. . . . In the following example the patriarch Arias Gonzalo offers his five sons to Urraca for the defense of Zamora against the troops of King Sancho:

Defenderánte el muro de Zamora	A
estos cinco renuevos arrancados	B
de este árbol verde, aunque marchito agora.	A
De apoyo servirán a mis cuidados,	B
que son tuyos, señora, si es que llego	C
a servir de caudillo a tus soldados.	B
Don Gonzalo, llegad; llegad, don Diego,	C
don Rodrigo y don Pedro, ya con brío	D
para ceñirse espada; harálo luego	C
el menor, que es don Arias; ya le crío,	D
y tal, que en el discurso de la guerra,	E
del que muriere ocupará el vacío. (II, 212ab)	D

(These five stems from this once flourishing tree, although it is withered now, will defend the walls of Zamora for you. They will serve as support for all my cares, which are yours too, if I should become the leader of your soldiers. Come, don Gonzalo, don Diego, don Rodrigo and don Pedro, for you are all eager to gird on your sword. The youngest son, don Arias, will soon do the same. I am now training him in the art of war so that he will take the place left vacant by anyone of them that falls.)

Lira. It is to be regretted that there is confusion with regard to this strophe, for the term *lira* is applied by some to certain stanzas of five lines, while others apply it to certain stanzas of six lines. The name *lira* comes from the first line of the opening stanza of Garcilaso de la Vega's *Canción Quinta:*

> *Si de mi baja lira*
> *tanto pudiese el son, que un momento*
> *aplacase la ira*
> *del animoso viento,*
> *y la furia del mar y el movimiento.*

(If only the sound of my unworthy lyre could do so much as to momentarily pacify the wrath of the spirited wind and the fury and motion of the sea.)

This Italian verse form with its rhyme *aBabB,* which was greatly favored by San Juan de la Cruz and Fray Luis de León, is sometimes called "Luis de León *quintilla.*" Many scholars, however, call the stanza just given a form of the *canción* (Italian *canzone*) and define the *lira* as a strophe of six lines of seven and eleven syllables with three rhymes. Two rhymes occur in the first four lines, and the last two lines are always a rhymed couplet. This is the definition which Morley and Bruerton accept, and it is the one which will be used in this study.

This strophe of six verses, which is rather important in Castro's plays, is found in fourteen authentic dramas, and its importance increased during the playwright's career. Castro makes use of eleven forms of this strophe. In the following example the rhyme is *aBaBcC:*

> *¡Qué terrible congoja!*
> *¡Qué furioso mortal desasosiego!*
> *¿Qué haré? Todo me enoja,*
> *todo soy pena y llanto y todo fuego;*
> *que este agravio importuno*
> *cuatro elementos ha juntado en uno.*   (II, 527a)

(What terrible anguish! What furious mortal unease! What shall I do? Everything drives me into a rage, my whole being is sorrow, tears and fire; for this importune affront has joined four elements into one.)

Three other forms of the *lira* which are frequently found in Castro are *abbacC, AabBCC* and *AbbAcC.*

Versos sueltos. This verse form, which in English poetry is called unrhymed or blank verse, is defined as hendecasyllables without rhyme, with each passage generally ending in a rhymed couplet. Since there was a growing tendency among Golden Age poets to insert rhymed couplets within each passage, Morley and Bruerton consider a passage with fewer than fifty percent of rhymed lines to be *versos sueltos.* If the percentage of rhymed lines exceeds the above figure, they classify it as *silva 3°.*

Versos sueltos are found in ten plays by Castro. The following is taken from a long passage found in *Mercy in Justice:*

> *Si yo conozco en mi naturaleza*
> *que se apasiona viendo la hermosura,*
> *¿extremo llaman a lo que es cordura?*
> *¿Podré ser buen juez, apasionado?*
> *Si una voz mujeril, cuando es señora,*
> *es lisonja del gusto y del oído,*
> *¿cómo se escaparán de apasionados*
> *los oídos de un rey lisonjeados?*
> *Déjalos, digan, digan, Feduardo,*
> *pues yo entiendo mejor que si en el mundo*
> *sin ver y sin oír a las mujeres*
> *todos los hombres como yo juzgaran,*
> *muchos inconvenientes se excusaran.* (III, 137b ff.)

(If I am aware that my own being becomes impassioned by the sight of beauty, do they call great extremes what is really wisdom? Can I be a good judge if I am impassioned? If a woman's voice, when it masters us, is pleasant and flattering to the ear, how can the flattered ears of a king escape being impassioned? Never mind, let them talk, Feduardo; for I understand better than they that if in this world all would judge as I do, without seeing or hearing women, many troubles would be avoided.)

Canción. This is a strophe with lines of seven and eleven syllables, and it may vary in length from five to twenty lines. The same rhyme scheme is generally found in each stanza of a passage. The following example is from *Cid I:*

> RODRIGO. *Suspenso de afligido*
> *estoy. Fortuna, ¿es cierto lo que veo?*
> *Tan en mi daño ha sido*
> *tu mudanza, que es tuya, y no la creo.*
> *¿Posible pudo ser que permitiese*
> *tu inclemencia que fuese*
> *mi padre el ofendido, ¡estraña pena!*
> *y el ofensor el padre de Ximena?* (II, 176b)

(RODRIGO. Overcome with grief, bewildered am I. Dame Fortune, is what I see true? So much to my perdition has been your inconstancy, yours alone, and I cannot believe it. Could it possibly have been permitted by your lack of compassion that my father should be the one dishonored and the offender the father of Jimena?)

The establishment of a fairly definite date of composition **for** the various works of an author is of considerable importance, especially in the matter of the evaluation of his growth as a writer. The date of publication of a volume of plays (*Parte*) is not always of help since some of the plays may have been written several years before the volume was published. In a few cases, however, objective criteria, such as topical references and well-reasoned assumptions, are the means by which the date of composition of some of Castro's plays can be inferred. For example, in *The Happy Revelation* (I, 341b), the shepherd Lisardo laments the death of Nísida. Juliá Martínez believes that Castro here has in mind the death of his first wife, doña Marquesa, which occurred probably shortly before 1600 (I, x). Bruerton assigns the date *ca.* 1599 to this play, which strengthens the suggestion offered by Juliá Martínez. Cervantes' *Don Quijote de la Mancha* enjoyed immediate popularity after the publication of its *Part One* in 1605, and it seems reasonable, as Bruerton suggests, that Castro's two plays, *Don Quijote from la Mancha* and *Dangerous Curiosity*, which are based on Cervantes' novel, were written shortly after its publication when the work's popularity was very high. The same reasoning suggests that Castro's *Kinship's Powerful Call*, which is based on Cervantes' *La fuerza de la sangre*, was written shortly after 1613, the year in which the *Novelas Ejemplares* were published.

Professor Ruth Lee Kennedy assigns a date probably after 1617 for *The Greatest Spouse*, that being the year in which the doctrine of the Immaculate Conception was formally recognized by Rome.[4] The date of composition given by Bruerton for this work is 1617–20? In *The Deceiver Deceived* there is a reference to *bigotera*, a device which young men of fashion wore in order to train their *bigote* (mustache). This device is referred to in the play as *obra nueva en España* ("something new in Spain") III, 171b. All indications point to 1611 or 1612 as the year in which *bigoteras* first appeared in Spain, with 1612 as the more likely date. The reference in the play to the device as "something new in Spain" suggests a date much earlier than Bruerton's 1622?–24.[5] Thus the probable date of composition of a few of Castro's plays over a period of nearly thirty years has been established, which will give some idea of the way in which certain strophes were becoming less popular and others were gaining in this dramatist's favor.

In his study of the chronology of Castro's plays, Bruerton states that since too few of his plays can be dated objectively, "It would therefore, have been impossible to contribute very much to the chronology of Castro's theatre had there not been available the voluminous material culled from Lope, as well as many data of other dramatists of the period" (p. 90). So after Morley and Bruerton had completed their monumental work on Lope de Vega, Bruerton applied the same technique to the versification of plays which he considered to be authentic Castro, and to other plays attributed to him. He finds that the playwright's use of *redondilla* is much more regular over the years than Lope's, but this strophe becomes less important as *romance* increases. Castro shows a preference for *type I quintilla*, but it too diminishes gradually in importance. *Décima* is one of his least-favored meters, while *romance* is found in all his dated plays and shows considerable increase in the later plays. His one form of *silva* is *silva 2°*. *Octavas* and sonnets are not highly favored. His early plays show a high percentage of *tercetos*. *Lira* tends to increase in percentage, and *canción* is found in both his early and late plays. Castro's dramas show a fairly definite ratio of percentages among the various meters at any given period, and this ratio shows a gradual change over the span of his literary career. The percentages in the three plays which Bruerton considers to be the dramatist's earliest are as follows:

Constant Love: Redondillas, 70.3; *quintillas*, 9.8; *décimas*, 1.1; *romance*, 7.1; *octavas*, 1.8; *tercetos*, 3.3; *lira*, 0.7; *sueltos*, 2.2; *canción*, 3.6.

The Happy Revelation: Redondillas, 58.7; *quintillas*, 18.8; *décimas*, 1.; *romance*, 4.2; *octavas*, 1.1; *tercetos*, 5.6; *liras*, 1.8; *sueltos*, 4.5; *canción*, 4.3.

The Birth of Montesinos: Redondillas, 58; *quintillas*, 33.8; *romance*, 3.9; *octavas*, 1.5; *sueltos*, 2.7.

The percentages for the two *Cid* plays, which were written approximately during the middle of Castro's literary career, show that *redondillas* decrease in importance as *romance* increases:

Cid II: Redondillas, 47.6; *quintillas*, 13.4; *romance*, 25.7; *octavas*, 3.6; *tercetos*, 8.4; *sueltos*, 1.2.

Cid I: Redondillas, 53.1; *quintillas*, 4; *décimas*, 2.3; *romance*, 31.4; *tercetos*, 2.5; *canción*, 0.8; *redondillas* and *quintillas*, alternating, 5.7.

The increase in the importance of *romance* is evident in the percentages for the last three of Bruerton's authentic plays:

How Much One Esteems One's Honor: Redondillas, 46.2; *décimas,* 11.7; *romance,* 32.4; *octavas,* 1.2; *liras,* 5.2; *canción,* 3.3.

The Deceiver Deceived: Redondillas, 43; *décimas,* 5.5; *romance,* 33.1; *silva 2°,* 3.1; *octavas,* 4.4; *sonnet,* 0.5; *liras,* 3.5; *canción,* 6.8.

The Impoverished Seeker of Royal Favor: Redondillas, 53.9; *décimas,* 4.6; *romance,* 41.5.

Bruerton's study of Castro's strophes is highly valuable in establishing the chronology of his plays. But the study also provides a feature of great importance—information with regard to the authenticity of many plays which Juliá Martínez has included in his three-volume edition. The three plays which Bruerton lists as "Probably by Castro" were not published in either of the dramatist's *Partes,* but the pattern of verse forms and the ratio of percentages conform to his practice. In the plays which are classified as "Doubtful," the verse evidence is inconclusive for *A Packet of Gray Hairs and Hesitant Revenge, His Father's Grandson, Faint Heart Never Won Fair Lady,* and *The Honorable Poor Nobleman.* The remaining four plays in this group show considerable deviation from authentic Castro. The same is true of the four plays which Bruerton classifies as "Texts not by Castro." [6]

CHAPTER 4

Guillén de Castro and the
Spanish Code of Honor

THREE concepts permeate the life and literature of Golden Age Spain—God, the King, and the Code of Honor. God was viewed from a strictly orthodox Roman Catholic perspective. The King was accepted as God's representative on earth, and Spaniards of those days believed firmly in his divine right to rule. Many people today can appreciate even if they cannot accept these beliefs in a Divine Ruler and His divinely appointed human representative. But modern man will find it difficult to appreciate or accept the third member of this trilogy—the Spanish concept of honor. Honor was an all-powerful concept that ruled and limited the actions of wellborn Spaniards, a concept that could, when least expected, result in the loss of face, provoke a duel, or cause a man to kill an innocent wife, daughter, or sister merely for the sake of appearances.

The high esteem in which honor was held is illustrated by an incident in the picaresque novel *Lazarillo de Tormes*, which was written in the first half of the sixteenth century. Lazarillo's third master, a squire, has given up a status of economic security in Old Castile and has come to Toledo where he suffers privation. His explanation is that he left his former home in order to avoid having to doff his hat first each time that he met a certain neighboring nobleman of higher rank. Since his neighbor was never courteous enough to doff his hat first occasionally, the squire considered that this was an affront on his honor, in which, he remarks to Lazarillo, is centered all that a gentleman considers to be of value. Lazarillo, in an aside to the Lord, comments on the great number of men like the squire who would endure greater suffering for their honor than they would for Him.

Numerous statements in Castro's plays reflect the high value which was placed on honor:

". . . men of high rank hold honor in greater esteem than life" (II, 114a).

"Where honor intervenes, all else stands for naught" (II, 445a).

"Honor takes preference over pleasure" (III, 268a).

"Alas, saintly honor, great is your worth but also great is your burden" (III, 65a).

"Any affront assumes gigantic proportions for a man of honor" (II, 178b).

In *The Birth of Montesinos,* Montesinos asks his father Grimaltos for a definition of honor: "And tell me, sir, what is honor?" Grimaltos replies: "It is a reputation for being held in esteem, known by man but not by its color. It is an invisible thing which is nourished by blood, and it is so voracious and terrible, that, unchecked and avid, it always aspires to the impossible. It never remains in one being, it can take away as well as give, and at times it goes about so unseen that it is not where it seems to be and it seems not to be where it really is. It is seen most where it is least in evidence, and it comes quietly so that no one can see it, and the one who least desires it is always most involved with it. In short, son, it is a fancied serious dark shadow, and in the world, which it keeps in suspense, it is the thing most talked about and the least known." Montesinos exclaims: "I don't quite understand it." To which Grimaltos responds: "Very few people understand it, but many are born with it" (I, 438b ff.).

Elsewhere in Castro's plays, one finds the following definitions of honor:

"Honor in the world, son, consists only of being held in high repute by others" (I, 50b).

". . . since honor consists of being held in high repute by others" (II, 120a).

When Montesinos asks his father how a man can lose his honor, the reply is that he can lose it by lying, stealing, showing cowardice, being a traitor, or becoming drunk with wine. Grimaltos says that a man can also lose his honor when someone tells him "You lie" or administers a buffet to him. Montesinos asserts that such a person would pay with his tongue or hand for such an outrage. But when his father adds that a man's wife can deprive him of honor, even if he is completely blameless, Montesinos asks what law is responsible for such a situation, and asserts that a man may become involved in great danger if he marries, for he entrusts his honor to a woman (I, 439ab).

A passage in *The Foolish Young Gentleman* (I, 50b ff.), repeats many expressions and statements concerning honor which are found in *The Birth of Montesinos...*

The late professor George T. Northup, in the excellent introduction to his edition of three plays by Calderón, has a section called "The Spanish Conception of Honor." [1] Northup states: "Most aspects of the honor problem had already been treated by Lope and his school. Calderón, with his legalistic mind, merely developed the idea and refined upon it. We may say that he codified honor" (p. xvi). Northup lists the following laws (*leyes*) or aphorisms which comprise the code of honor as exemplified in Calderón's plays: *La ley natural* ("the law of self-defense"), which gave an individual the right to protect himself even when attacked by the king; *La ley de la presencia real* ("the law of the royal presence"), which implied that there must be no dueling in the presence of the king or in the royal palace, and if the king should happen to come upon a duel, it must cease at once and must not be renewed; *Galanteo en palacio* ("courtship in the royal palace"), proscribed because it was considered to be an insult to the queen; *Haciendo el agravio deudo* ("taking the wrong into the family"), meaning that the marriage of even very distant relatives of the two antagonists brought to an end any serious differences between them which could cause a duel, since, according to the code, one kinsman must not do wrong to another kinsman; *Con quien vengo, vengo* ("I stand by the man I am with"), which obligated a man to help his friend in his quarrels.

One's own safety or honor, however, came first according to the law *primero soy yo* ("I come first"), except in the case of a woman, for whom great sacrifices could be demanded by *antes que todo es mi dama* ("my lady takes precedence over all"). Strangers could ask for help or sanctuary by means of the formula, *por forastero* ("because I am a stranger"). This was especially true of ladies in distress whose plea *por mujer y desdichada* ("because I am a woman in need of help") obligated any nobleman to come to her aid.

It was mentioned earlier that a man could lose his honor because of a *bofetón* (buffet) from an enemy. But this did not apply if the buffet was delivered by a woman, because *las blancas manos no ofenden* ("white hands cannot deprive a man of his honor"). It was taken for granted that there would be considerable deceiving and duplicity in love affairs according to the formula *amor es todo enredos* ("anything is fair in love"). The importance of keeping the loss of one's honor from becoming known in public is stressed by *no hay cosa como callar* ("secrecy is the best solution") and *a secreto agravio, secreta venganza* ("for a secret offense, a secret revenge").

Thus the Spanish code of honor, similar to any code, was a collection of laws, many of them unwritten. But one unresolved problem relating to honor as it is dealt with in Spanish literature of the Golden Age was, "When did the use of the word *ley* (law) with reference to certain aspects of honor become sufficiently common so that one could say that honor had become codified? In spite of Northup's assertion that Calderón codified honor, one can find in Castro's plays references which show that honor had either become codified or was becoming codified at least several years before Calderón's first play was written. In *The Happy Revelation* (I, 328b) which, according to Bruerton, is one of Castro's earliest plays "*ca.* 1599," and in *The Birth of Montesinos* (I, 419b) one finds specific mention of *la ley de amistad* ("the law of friendship"). According to this law, neither friends nor acquaintances had the right to intervene in or attempt to break up a courtship of long standing. This law, incidentally, is not included in Northup's list. Additional instances of the use of the word "law" with respect to certain aspects of honor are found in nine plays by Castro which Bruerton dates 1605 or earlier.[2] Here is support for the statement that the codification of honor was well under way several years before Calderón's first play appeared.

The divine right of kings is an exceedingly important aspect of the code of honor. Typical of the general acceptance of the king as God's representative on earth are the following quotations from Castro's plays:

"If just kings represent the semblance and government of God on earth . . ." (II, 192b).

"What are you doing? Sir, kings should not be like other men; because, as in Heaven, they are the Prime Mover on earth" (III, 312a).

KING. "The cause is not mine: the justice which I dispense is of

God; His is the strong cutting sword unsheathed by Him in my hand" (III, 150b).

A corollary of the divine right of kings was the duty of the vassal to render complete obedience to his ruler:

"The faithful vassal must obey his king in everything" (II, 12a).

"For in a vassal obedience to the king must always be mute and blind" (III, 301a).

"For he is my God-given Lord, and it is an honor for a vassal to hasten to obey him" (II, 224a).

But according to Castro, there was one exception to the demands of complete obedience to one's king. Don Miguel Centellas pointedly reminds the King of Naples of this exception when he tells him, "for only when it is a question of marriage may a man with honor fail to do the king's pleasure" (II, 160b).

There was a strange bond which kept intact loyalty to one's king and which protected the ruler from harm even in cases in which physical violence to his person would seem to be justified.

As a rule, neither the king nor a prince could deprive a subject of honor by delivering a blow. In *The Foolish Young Gentleman,* for example, Prince Lotario, in a pique of anger, slaps the face of a duke. The latter's hotheaded young son, Anteo, vows that he will kill the prince for having dishonored his father. Anteo's brother admonishes him that their father had not been deprived of his honor according to the code, for a prince delivered the blow in the presence of the king. Anteo replies that "There is no loss of honor if he punishes, but there is if he affronts a person" (I, 61a).

But subjects found themselves in an alarming dilemma when there was a question of defending a female relative whose honor had been threatened by a member of the royal family. Northup, in his discussion of honor obligations between king and subject, states that a king "can dishonor a female subject by seducing her, and thereby offend her male relatives. Theoretically, these have the right to erase the wrong by shedding the royal blood, but this situation (it occurs in *La vida es sueño*) is never courageously met in the *comedia*. Instead of taking drastic action, the offended one battles with his wits and finds an ingenious solution" (pp. xvii ff.).

Seeking an ingenious solution may be true in the case of Calderón and some other dramatists of the Golden Age, but it is not true of Guillén de Castro, some of whose characters resort to drastic action in such a situation. The king in *Constant Love* attempts to seduce Nísida. Her father, a duke, with sword drawn prevents him from doing so. The king then grasps his sword and strikes the duke on the head. One can note a fine distinction between the defense of one's honor and the defense of one's person when both are attacked by royalty, as the duke tells the king to strike him if he wishes, for he will not defend his body against any blow delivered by him since it belongs to both the king and himself, but he will defend his honor against the king because his honor is his alone (I, 15a).

In *Proud Humility*, when a prince attempts to force his attentions upon the fiancée of don Juan, the latter warns the prince: "Don't touch her, or I will take down my sword. . . . I do not offend my king in this, because I am defending my honor" (I, 476b). A similar situation occurs in *Mentor to his Son*, a play which Bruerton considers to be probably by Castro. A duke, defending the honor of a female resident of his household against a prince who is trying to seduce her, emphatically reminds him that there is a limit to the prerogatives of royalty, and that he would defend with his sword any attempt by the king himself to tarnish his honor (III, 461b ff.).

There are in Castro's plays suggestions that a tyrannical king can be repudiated by his subjects:

"For a king can be deprived of his title as soon as he becomes a tyrant" (I, 14b).

"For a king ceases to be king as soon as he becomes a tyrant" (III, 130b).

It is evident that Castro does not follow slavishly the doctrine of the divine right of kings. This is especially true in two cases of regicide which occur in his plays, and which could well have brought down upon him the wrath of the royal family as well as ecclesiastical censure. The cruel tyrannical king in *Constant Love* is killed by his nephew Leonido in full view of the audience. José María Roca comments upon this action: "We find ourselves, then, faced with a revolutionary work, both in its exposition and in its dénouement. If the dramatists of our Golden Age occasionally dare to discuss the royal authority, they never go as far as the Valencian poet. Guillén de Castro not only discusses it but he sanctions its discussion, and what is more, he presents the assassin on the stage with the greatest distinction." [3]

This daring breach of the code is palliated to a certain extent by the king's remarks to Leonido as he looks upon the corpses of two of his victims: "So be it; for I am in such a state now as I view myself here, that I even give you permission to kill me" (I, 44b). His death at the hands of Leonido ensues immediately as the young avenger exclaims that he accepts the permission to kill.

Castro's second case of regicide is found in *The Perfect Knight*, when Ludovico kills the king in order to prevent him from murdering the queen. This drastic action is palliated by the fact that the king's father had acceded to the throne by killing the rightful ruler, and hence his tyrannical son was not Ludovico's God-given king (II, 167b).

Castro gives us other references to the relations between king and subject. There must be no dueling in the king's presence nor in the royal palace (I, 369b: II, 202b; III, 10a). In *Cid I*, when the young Rodrigo kills Count Lozano in a duel at the very doors of the palace, King Fernando angrily exclaims: "To kill the count almost within my sight bordered on treason" (II, 182b). The king seems not so much upset by the fact that Count Lozano was killed as he is by where he was killed.

Courtship in the royal palace was also proscribed because it supposedly showed lack of respect for the queen. Thus, in *Constant Love*, when the king comes upon two lovers in his palace, he remarks: "What, is such shamelessness fitting for my palace? . . . This is taking too great a liberty" (I, 11a). Don Miguel Centellas, Castro's "Perfect Knight," who is living in the king's palace, refuses to engage in a surreptitious courtship there as he asserts: "But consider whether it is loyal, whether it is just, whether it is right, for me to marry like a thief in the palace of the king" (II, 147b).

Quotations have been given earlier in this chapter which state that "men of high rank hold honor in greater esteem than life," "where honor intervenes, all else stands for naught," and "honor takes preference over pleasure." Consequently, the loss of honor had genuinely tragic implications for a nobleman, implications which persisted until the lost honor was restored in one way or another. Diego Laínez, the decrepit father of Rodrigo de Vivar, the Cid to be, suffers the loss of honor when the lusty Count Lozano slaps his face in the presence of King Fernando and a few courtiers. Diego Laínez remarks to those who have witnessed the affront: "Since I am left without honor, and he, haughty and in high spirits, takes with him added to the honor which he already had, the honor which he has taken from me, I will go away if I am able, stumbling with each step over the burden of my affront and the weight of my years, to a place where I can weep over my grievance until I can be avenged" (II, 173a).

According to the code, an affront to the honor of one member of a family affected all the other members. Since Diego Laínez was too old and feeble to regain his lost honor by himself, the obligation to restore the family honor devolved upon his son Rodrigo, who challenged the redoubtable count to a duel and killed him. As Diego Laínez sends Rodrigo forth to erase the blemish on the family honor, he reminds him: "And this blemish on my honor, which touches your own, wash it away with blood, for blood alone removes such blemishes" (II, 176a). Rodrigo's father later tells how he reacted when he saw his enemy lying dead upon the ground: "I went over, and I found him dead, so with a spirit no longer troubled, I put my heart into my affront and my fingers into his wound. With blood I washed the place where the blemish was to be found, because honor which is washed clean must be washed with blood" (II, 182a).

Except for the use of the blood of an enemy as an ablution, this scene is typical of the way in which many affairs of honor between noblemen were settled in the Golden Age. Differences could be adjusted and a duel could thus be avoided by means of an apology, but examples of such procedure are extremely rare. Shortly after Diego Laínez had been dishonored by Count Lozano, a friend of the count suggested that he apologize, but the latter refused to do so, asserting that an apology would dishonor him and would not restore the lost honor of Diego Laínez; the best solution is to settle affronts by means of the sword (II, 177b ff.).

It was of paramount importance to do all within one's power to prevent the loss of honor from becoming publicly known: "An affront which is kept from being known does not dishonor one in fact" (I, 326a). "Secret offenses are avenged in secret" (II, 478b). King Fernando stressed the importance of secrecy in such matters when he admonished the courtiers who witnessed Count Lozano's act of aggression against Diego Laínez: "Since the unfortunate affair took place in my closed room and the secret is safe, let no one dare to make it public" (II, 173a).

Two indispensable parts of a young nobleman's accoutrement during the Golden Age were a cloak and a sword (*capa y espada*). Having such a lethal weapon as a sword within reach of one's hand frequently resulted in swordplay when hotheaded young men of the time were faced with a real or fancied assault upon their honor. A similar situation existed in this country in the old Wild West when practically every man went armed with a revolver. Anyone who has read widely in literature of the Golden Age cannot help but be impressed by the numerous instances of duels. In an article which equates honor and dueling, William J. Entwistle refers to "the laws of the duel, because these are the ones which governed all the attitudes of the nobleman in contact with his peers." [4] Duels between noblemen were frequently precipitated by the blunt assertion *¡Mentís!* or *¡Tú mientes!* ("You lie!"). Such an insult, uttered by one whose sword was sheathed, left the offended person no recourse except swordplay in order to wash away with blood the blemish on his honor. But if one drew his sword before shouting "You lie!" his adversary's honor was not impugned: "The drawing of the sword was an acknowledgement that the drawer considered his adversary an equal, brave, and ready to resent a wrong. These flattering implications mitigated, even if they did not cancel, the insult." [5] Thus, when the perfidious Tomillas, whose honor has already been affronted, tells Grimaltos "You lie!" Grimaltos counters with the statement that a "You lie!" from a person who has lost his honor cannot affront anyone, especially when it is uttered with the sword drawn (I, 422b).

Although duels play an important part in many of Castro's dramas, the playwright gives us only piecemeal comments about this important aspect of the honor code. The one who has been challenged has the right to choose the place for the duel and the weapons (III, 71b). The antagonists strip to the waist (III, 72b), and their swords are measured for length before the start of the duel (I, 364a). As a rule, there should be no dueling in the presence of women, "because tongues and swords owe great respect to women and to elders" (II, 295a). But one can find instances in Castro's plays in which duels either took place in the presence of women or in which the antagonists were restrained only with great difficulty (II, 264a; II, 310b; III, 102b).

Honor was generally considered to be the patrimony of the nobility, and consequently it was not deemed fitting for members of that class to duel with their inferiors. But there was also an element of practicality in this taboo. If a nobleman should draw his sword in combat with an inferior, the nobleman must show that he excels his foe in bravery as well as in social status. Unless he kills or routs his antagonist, or dies in the attempt, his reputation will suffer and he will be the object of gossip, perhaps slander. So for these reasons, if he can possibly do so, a nobleman must overlook anything which could provoke a duel with a nonnoble (III, 47a).

In the case of a challenge to a duel which has been issued because of a misunderstanding, and the misunderstanding is explained satisfactorily, it would seem that the explanation would obviate any recourse to swordplay. But such was not always the case. In one instance, a young man who has been challenged and who has given a satisfactory explanation for the misunderstanding insists upon going on with the duel. His reason is that one who has been challenged to a duel can hardly return to town without killing or being killed (III, 671a). The play in which this scene occurs is of doubtful attribution to Castro. Similar instances of the necessity to fight a duel in spite of the giving of satisfactory explanation are found in *Faint Heart Never Won Fair Lady* (III, 493b), and in Ruiz de Alarcón's *La verdad sospechosa* (*Suspicious Truth*), Act II, Scene xi. These examples indicate the powerful influence of *el qué dirán* ("what will people say?") as part of the honor code.

In contrast with some of the barbaric aspects of the law of the duel were certain cases in which fair play was prescribed. A man who drops his weapon in the course of a duel is given the opportunity to regain it (III, 10a). A nobleman does not take an unfair advantage of an enemy by having his friends help him (I, 332a), and he will help another who is being attacked by more than one person (III, 178b). A nobleman, in trying to prevent a duel, warns the antagonists that he will go to the aid of the nonaggressor (I, 25b). In *Proud Humility*, don Rodrigo, a formidable swordsman, is challenged by don Diego, who is relatively inexperienced in dueling. Not wishing to have an unfair advantage,

Rodrigo tells him to learn how to wound, vanquish, and kill, and when he has mastered the art of fighting then he can cross swords with him (I, 489b). An army captain, secretly watching a young friend who is a novice at dueling pit his lack of experience against an experienced antagonist, makes up his mind not to help him unless he is attacked treacherously or attacked by more than one opponent (III, 72a).

It was stated at the beginning of this chapter that modern man will find it difficult to appreciate or accept the Golden Age concept of honor. This is especially true insofar as woman is concerned: "Spanish honor was based fundamentally, on the woman: on her modesty, chastity and virtue. And based on her was her own honor as well as that of the male: the husband's, on the married woman; the father's, or in his absence, the brother's, on that of the unmarried woman, the daughter or sister.

"Feminine honor is the center of gravity, the basis of social cohesion. On the honor of the woman rests the community of the family, that of family lines and lineage, that of the entire body politic." [6]

Since the slightest breach of decorum on the part of a woman could involve her close male relatives in the dangerous process of regaining her lost honor, women were kept under surveillance. If they ventured into the street, it was only when heavily veiled and accompanied by a male member of the family or friend of the family, or by some elderly male or female servant. This mistrust of women was compounded by the fact that they were considered to be lacking in intellect and integrity. Woman is referred to in *Don Quijote de la Mancha* as "an imperfect animal." This disparaging belief was of long standing and received wide acceptation during the Golden Age. [7]

A woman's lost honor could be restored by marriage, "taking the affront into the family," after which bygones were bygones. This is the typical solution of the problem in most cape-and-sword plays. A less happy solution was the shedding of blood, either that of the male culprit or that of the woman involved, or that of both parties. There are cases in the drama in which the sacrifice of a woman who is completely innocent of wrongdoing seems to be the only way to solve a man's honor dilemma, and this for the mere reason that she was caught in the web of circumstances. Such is the dilemma which faces don Miguel Centellas, Castro's

"Perfect Knight," who mistakenly believes that his honor has been affronted by his father, his king, and his wife. Loyalty prevents him from seeking redress from his father or from his king. So he decides that the only hope which is left to him to regain his lost honor is to shed the blood of his wife (II, 166ab). The constable in *Ingratitude Caused by Love* has good reason to suspect that the king is trying to force his attentions upon his wife. Uncertain as to whether or not his wife is involved, the unhappy man decides that she must die whether she is innocent or guilty in order that his honor may remain unsullied (III, 521b).

The classic example in Spanish drama of the sacrifice of an innocent woman in order to preserve her husband's honor free from blemish is Calderón de la Barca's *El médico de su honra* (*The Physician of his Honor*). In this play, the woman, falsely accused of infidelity, is forced by her husband to let a practitioner slit her veins, which causes her to bleed to death.[8] One is surprised by the rather numerous examples of women in the Golden Age drama who willingly accept immolation because of some real or fancied blemish on their honor. The tyrannical king in *Constant Love*, who has repudiated his wife, gives Nísida the choice of marriage to him or death by poison. She prefers death to dishonor. As she drinks the poison, her father tells her: "Daughter, you will be the bright mirror of pure honor" (I, 35b). In another play, a woman who believes that the presence of a strange man in her room has deprived her of honor, hands a dagger to her husband and asks him to kill her (II, 89a).

Occasionally the question arises in Castro's plays as to whether a woman, who has been seduced by force, has suffered an affront upon her honor, and if so, should she be put to death? Such is the dilemma which confronts Teosindo when he learns that his wife Filomena has been ravished and mutilated by King Tereo. He meditates upon the problem: "But how can I blame her for violence on the part of the king? But the rigor of the law says that I have been affronted. . . . Where there is no guilt can there be an affront? What inflexible severity! But it is a stain which is due to misfortune or deceit, and although the cloth is not to blame, the suit cannot be worn" (I, 143a).

In view of the barbarous and inflexible aspects of many of the laws which made up the honor code, it is not surprising that some writers of the Golden Age did voice their condemnation. One finds throughout the works of Cervantes, for example, numerous allusions to many of the cruel and un-Christian aspects of the code,[9] and one of his *Exemplary Tales, La fuerza de la sangre* (*Kinship's Powerful Call*), goes directly counter to the principle that a woman who has been dishonored by force should suffer death at the hands of her father or at those of some other close male relative. In this story, after Leocadia has been raped and released by Rodolfo, she finds her way home. Tearfully explaining to her parents what has happened, she asks her father to put her to death. Her father reminds her that she has not offended God by word, thought, or deed, and consoles her with the assurance that in the sight of God she can live in honor. He also tells her that he will ever look upon her as a loving father should.[10]

For some strange reason, Guillén de Castro is rarely mentioned as one of the writers who protested against the cruelty and inflexibility of the honor code. But the fact is that he expressed criticism that is just as vehement as that which was expressed by Cervantes, Lope, and Calderón. In his adaptation of Cervantes' exemplary novel, *Kinship's Powerful Call*, he accepts the novelist's thesis that a woman who has been seduced by force has not been deprived of her honor. Castro is especially critical of the fact that a man's honor may depend on such a frail thing as a woman: "Alas, women! What legal absolutism can bind us to the certainty that one who cannot give honor can take it away?" (II, 15b). "A plague upon the man who trusts in the honor and loyalty of women" (II, 525a). "What law, without astounding the world, managed to place all the honor of a man in the hands of a woman?" (III, 529a).

Although honor assumes an important role in the plays of Guillén de Castro, he does not give us as complete a picture of the code as Calderón de la Barca does. This is explained in part by the smaller number of plays written by Castro. Some aspects of the code as found in Calderón seem truly incredible and puerile to modern man. For example: a blow administered by the king to a subject could not be resented, but an innocent bystander who witnessed the blow thereby offended the recipient, with the result that the two would have to fight a duel. In a similar fashion, if a woman spoke insulting words to a man, words which happened to be heard by another male, a duel would have to take place, but only later, because duels should not be fought in the presence of a lady.[11]

Such, then, was the Golden Age code of honor, for the most part barbaric in essence, but with at least an occasional leaven of humanity and sportsmanship. Two questions which frequently arise in connection with the code are, "What was its origin?" and "Why did it assume such importance in Spain and not in the other countries of Western Europe?" There are many features of the honor code which seem to have been implanted by the Moors during their long stay in the Iberian Peninsula. One can mention in this respect the close watch kept over women, their venturing forth into the streets only when heavily veiled and in the company of a member of the family, a friend of the family, or an elderly servant. The clan spirit with the motto, "An injury to one is an injury to all," and the powerful impulse to save face by wiping away affronts to one's honor by the shedding of blood also seem to have something Moorish and Oriental about them. One should also bear in mind that the history of Spain differs from the history of other European nations in that Spain is the only country in Western Europe in which the Moors were able to hold sway for centuries—they entered the country in 711 A.D. and were not expelled until 1492—nearly eight hundred years later. The Spanish code of honor also seems to reflect the influence of the Germanic tribes which invaded the country early in the fifth century. Great too, was the influence of the Jews, who were an important group in the nation until their expulsion early in the Renaissance.[12]

The belief is often held that "honor" was the patrimony of the upper classes. Northup, for example, asserts that the honor code "hampered the actions of the wellborn Spaniard in all his human relationships." [13] In equating "honor" and "duel," Entwistle expresses the opinion that the laws of the duel governed all the attitudes of the man of the upper classes in contact with his equals, and "honor" belonged exclusively to the nobility and not to the man of the lower classes.[14] Gustavo Correa, on the other hand, mentions a double aspect of honor in the seventeenth century—"vertical honor" for royalty and nobility, and "horizontal honor" for those who were excluded from the privileges of the upper classes. "Vertical honor" existed by virtue of birth or outstanding merit, while "horizontal honor" referred to the complex social relationships of the nation as a whole.[15] Correa asserts that one did not have to belong to the upper classes in order to have a lively feeling of personal honor which tended to equalize the members of the entire community in spite of the class barriers. This explains the numerous plays which stress the great drive exerted by "honor" upon peasants.

A final question arises—was the honor code merely a literary convention or does it reflect current practices of society in the Golden Age? If one applies the adage "Where there is smoke there is fire," and if one bears in mind the important role that honor plays in the works of such important writers as Cervantes, Lope de Vega, and Calderón as well as in the works of numerous writers of lesser standing, it seems reasonable to assume that the code reflects more than a semblance of reality. The rather frequent adverse comments by many of these writers and by a host of theologians on the cruelty and un-Christian aspects of the code add strength to this assumption. Northup states that history records numerous honor murders.[16] C. A. Jones expresses the opinion that "the theme of honour in the plays is not a complete fiction, and that there were cases in real life similar to those which occurred in the theatre, where we know them as cases of honour." [17] Jones bases his belief upon the frequent condemnations of moralists of the time, but he seems to underestimate the important role played by honor when he asserts, "In my opinion the code of honour in the Spanish drama of the Golden Age is a convention which, although not entirely divorced from reality or morals, is closely concerned with neither of these things . . ." (p. 206).[18]

CHAPTER 5

The Two Cid Plays of Guillén de Castro

GUILLÉN de Castro is assured of a permanent place in Spanish literature for having been the first to dramatize the Cid legend. In the first half of the seventeenth century, the French dramatist Pierre Corneille based his play *Le Cid* on Castro's *Cid I*. *Le Cid* was the first tragedy with a modern theme in French literature, and is often referred to as "The cornerstone of French drama." As a result of Corneille's adaptation of *Cid I*, Guillén de Castro has become the best known in world literature of all the minor dramatists of the Spanish Golden Age.

Rodrigo de Vivar, the Cid, has played such an important role in the history and literature of Spain that one can speak of five "Cids": (1) The Cid of history; (2) The Cid of the epic poem; (3) The Cid of the chronicles; (4) The Cid of the ballads; and (5) The Cid of the drama. The Cid of the drama is best represented by Castro's two plays. This dramatist certainly had no direct contact with historical sources based on the life of Rodrigo de Vivar. Neither did he have any direct contact with the epic poem, which was not edited and made available to the public until 1779. He was undoubtedly familiar with some of the chronicles which dealt with the Cid, but it is in the ballads where he found the chief sources for his two plays. The skillful way in which he selected and blended this material will be evident in the sections which follow.

I   *Las mocedades del Cid* (*Comedia Primera*)
(*The Youthful Deeds of the Cid—Cid I*)

As the play opens, young Rodrigo de Vivar is about to be dubbed knight by King Fernando before the altar of Santiago in the presence of a few members of the royal family and several members of the nobility. King Fernando is not only his sponsor, but also will provide weapons for his protégé. After the customary three taps on the shoulder have been delivered, Princess Urraca, who is in love with Rodrigo, puts on his spurs for him and the Queen promises to furnish him with a horse. This scene is based on part of a ballad which is incorporated into Castro's *Cid II*. In this ballad Urraca rebukes Rodrigo:

Begone, Begone, Rodrigo, you arrogant Castilian, for you should be reminded of that time long passed when you became a knight at the altar of Santiago, when the king was your sponsor, and you, Rodrigo, his protégé: my father gave you the weapons, my mother gave you the horse, I put on your spurs for you so that you would be more honored.[1]

(*Afuera, afuera, Rodrigo, el soberbio castellano, acordársete debría de aquel tiempo ya pasado cuando fuiste caballero en el altar de Santiago, cuando el rey fue tu padrino, tú, Rodrigo, el ahijado: mi padre te dió las armas, mi madre te dió el caballo, yo te calcé las espuelas porque fueses más honrado.*)

After the ceremony, in a session of state with Rodrigo's father Diego Laínez, Count Lozano, and two other courtiers, the king appoints Diego Laínez to be the tutor of Prince Sancho. Count Lozano, angered because he had expected to receive that appointment, after a bitter argument, slaps the face of Diego Laínez, thus depriving him of honor. The dishonored courtier goes home, and realizing that he is too old and decrepit to duel with the young and vigorous count, decides to test his three sons in order to see which one of them he will select to regain the family honor. The two younger sons quail in the face of the slight physical pain inflicted upon them by their father, and he judges them to be unworthy. But when Diego Laínez tests Rodrigo by grasping his hand and biting one of his fingers, the latter's angry and violent reaction convinces his father that his oldest son has the mettle to stand up against the count. The dramatist bases this episode on a well-known ballad, paraphrasing most of it, but following it fairly closely in at least a few lines in which Rodrigo almost threatens his father:

Castro	Ballad
Let go, my father, plague take you! Let go and may you be	Let go, my father, plague you. Let go, and may you be damned,

damned! If you were not my father I would deal you a blow.

(¡Padre, soltad en mal hora!
¡Soltad, padre, en hora mala!
¡Si no fuérades mi padre
diéraos una bofetada! . . .)
                    (II, 176a)

for if you were not my father,
words would not give satisfaction,
and with my very own hand I
would pluck out your entrails . . .
(—Soltedes, padre, en mal hora,
Soltedes en hora mala, que a
no ser padre, no hiciera satis-
facción de palabras, antes con
la mano mesma vos sacara las
entrañas . . .)[2]

Rodrigo, informed of the deed which has dishonored all the members of the family, is torn between his filial duty and his love for Count Lozano's daughter, Jimena. Filial duty prevails over love. The young man, who as yet has not engaged in a duel, muses over the arduous task which confronts him in demanding satisfaction from the formidable count:

Castro	Ballad
What am I thinking of? Since my valor exceeds my years, in order to avenge my father by killing Count Lozano, of what matter is the fearful armed band of my powerful adversary, even if he has in the mountains a thousand Asturian friends? And does it matter that in the court of King Fernando of Leon his voice is the first, as is his arm in war? All that is little and nothing in the reparation of an affront, the first ever committed against the blood of Laín Calvo. Heaven will prosper me if the earth provides a place to duel, although this is the first time that I trust my valor to my right arm. I will bear this ancient sword of Mudarra the Castilian, although it is dull and rust-covered since the death of its great owner; and if I lose respect for it, I want it to accept as explanation of my gird-	The Cid was deep in thought, considering how young he was to gain revenge for his father by killing Count Lozano. He thought of the fearful armed band of his powerful adversary, who had there in the mountains a thousand Asturian friends; he considered how in the court of good King Fernando his voice was the first as was his arm in war. All seems but little to him compared to that affront, the first ever committed against the blood of Laín Calvo. He asks of Heaven, justice, and of the earth, a place to duel, of his father, permission to duel, and of honor, a strong right arm. . . . He took down an ancient sword of Mudarra the Castilian, which was old and rust-covered since the death of its great owner; and thinking that it alone was sufficient explanation, before he

ing it on in anger the words that I tell it in my agitation: Bear in mind, brave sword, that another Mudarra bears you, and he fights with my right arm for his greatly debased honor. I well know that you will feel shame over coming into my control, but shame you will never feel over seeing me take a step backward. As strong as your steel you will see me in the lists; you have acquired a second owner who is the equal of the first, for if some one should defeat me, vexed over that baleful deed, up to your hilt in my heart I will hide you out of shame.

(*¿Qué imagino? Pues que tengo más valor que pocos años, para vengar a mi padre, matando al conde Lozano, ¿qué importa el bando temido del poderoso contrario, aunque tenga en las montañas mil amigos asturianos? Y ¿qué importa que en la corte del rey de León, Fernando, sea su voto el primero, y en guerra el mejor su brazo? Todo es poco, todo es nada en descuento de un agravio, el primero que se ha hecho a la sangre de Laín Calvo. Daráme el cielo ventura, si la tierra me da campo, aunque es la primera vez que doy el valor al brazo. Llevaré esta espada vieja de Mudarra el castellano, aunque está bota y mohosa por la muerte de su amo; y si le pierdo el respeto, quiero que admita en descargo del ceñírmela ofendido, lo que la digo turbado: Haz cuenta, valiente espada, que otro Mudarra te ciñe, y que con mi brazo riñe por su honra maltratada. Bien sé*)

girded it on, he speaks to it in agitation;—Bear in mind, brave sword, that my arm is Mudarra's, and that you fight with his arm because the affront is his. I know that you will feel shame from seeing yourself thus in my hand; but shame you will never feel of seeing me withdraw one step. As strong as your steel you will see me in the lists; the equal of the first is the second owner whom you have acquired; and if someone defeats you, angered over that baleful deed, up to the hilt in my heart I will hide you in my fury.

(*Pensativo estaba el Cid viéndose de pocos años, para vengar a su padre matando al conde Lozano. Miraba el bando temido del poderoso contrario, que tenía en las montañas mil amigos asturianos: Miraba cómo en las Cortes del rey de León Fernando era su voto el primero, y en guerras mejor su brazo. Todo le parece poco respecto de aquel agravio, el primero que se ha fecho a la sangre de Laín Calvo. Al cielo pide justicia, a la tierra pide campo, al viejo padre licencia, y a la honra esfuerzo y brazo. . . . Descolgó una espada vieja de Mudarra el castellano, que estaba vieja y mohosa por la muerte de su amo: y pensando que ella sola bastaba para el descargo, antes que se la ciñese, así le dice turbado:—Faz cuenta, valiente espada, que es de Mudarra mi brazo, y que con su brazo riñes, porque suyo es el agravio. Bien sé que te correrás de verte así en la mi mano; mas no*)

que te correrás de venir a mi
poder, mas no te podrás correr
de verme echar paso atrás. Tan
fuerte como tu acero me verás en
campo armado; segundo dueño
has cobrado tan bueno como el
primero, pues cuando alguno me
venza, corrido del torpe hecho,
hasta la cruz en mi pecho te esconderé, de vergüenza.)
(II, 176b ff.).

te podrás correr de volver atrás
un paso. Tan fuerte como tu acero
me verás en campo armado; tan
bueno como el primero segundo
dueño has cobrado, y cuando
alguno te venza, del torpe fecho
enojado, fasta la cruz en mi pecho
te esconderé muy airado.)[3]

In the next scene, near the royal palace, Peransules, a friend of
Count Lozano, suggests that he apologize for his rash act, but the
count refuses to do so, saying that a duel is the only way in which
Diego Laínez can gain satisfaction for his lost honor. Rodrigo enters, and after he upbraids Count Lozano, the two leave the stage
to engage in a duel, much to the consternation of Urraca and
Jimena. The count, offstage, cries out that he has been done to
death. Some of his followers threaten Rodrigo, but Urraca comes
to his aid as the first act ends.

In Act II, Jimena and Diego have audience with King Fernando. Jimena is carrying a handkerchief stained with the blood
of her father, and Diego has smeared his cheek with the blood
of his enemy, thus washing away the stain on his honor. Jimena
demands justice for her father's death; Diego Laínez offers to die
for Rodrigo's deed, since his son had killed the count at the behest
of his father. When the king orders that Diego Laínez be imprisoned, Prince Sancho objects so vociferously to having his tutor
suffer such humiliation that the king releases Diego Laínez to the
custody of Sancho. In the meantime, Rodrigo has gone to the
home of Jimena, and when she returns from the palace he hands
her a dagger as he tells her to kill him with it. In a highly melodramatic scene, the two discuss the reasons for their actions, the
scene ending with Jimena's admission that although she loves
Rodrigo, whom she has called her "adored enemy," honor forces
her to persecute him.

Rodrigo's father has assembled an army of five hundred soldiers
and advises his son to lead them into battle against the Moors who
are devastating much territory in Castile. Specifically mentioned
as suffering from attack by the heathens are Burgos, Montes de

Oca, Logroño, and Belforado. In addition to material destruction, many Christians have been taken prisoner. Here Castro has paraphrased the first few lines of a ballad: "Moorish kings enter Castile with great hue and cry; of the Moors five are kings and the rest commoners. They passed close to Burgos, they have overrun Montes de Oca, and raiding Belforado and Santo Domingo, Nájera and Logroño as well, they have destroyed everything. They are carrying away a booty of cattle, many Christian captives, men, women, and also boys and girls."

> (*Reyes moros en Castilla*
> *entran con gran alarido;*
> *de moros son cinco reyes,*
> *lo demás mucho gentío.*
> *Pasaron por junto a Burgos,*
> *A Montes-d'Oca han corrido,*
> *y corriendo a Belforado,*
> *también a Santo Domingo,*
> *a Nájera y a Logroño,*
> *todo lo habían destruido.*
> *Llevan presa de ganados,*
> *muchos cristianos cautivos,*
> *hombres muchos y mujeres,*
> *y también niñas y niños.*) [4]

    As Rodrigo leads his troops past the queen's summer home, Urraca summons him, and after suggesting that he could be a suitable match for her in spite of the difference in their rank, she gives him her blessing as he leaves to confront the enemy. The battle scene is described by a shepherd who, from a place of safety tells how the Christians approach, join battle with the infidels and rout them. Outstanding is the Christian leader who kills Moors as one would kill flies and who, after capturing one of the kings of the enemy, vows to capture three others that very day. Castro bases this in part on a few additional lines of the ballad just quoted: "When Rodrigo learned of this in his castle in Vivar, while still quite young and not yet twenty, he mounts his horse and his friends mount theirs; he sent out an appeal to the land, many people have joined him; he launched a great attack against the Moors: in the castle of Montes de Oca he defeated all the Moors and took the five kings prisoner."

(Rodrigo cuando lo supo
en Vivar, el su castillo,
mozo es de pocos días,
los veinte años no ha cumplido,
cabalga sobre Babieca,
y con él sus amigos:
apellidara a la tierra;
mucha gente le ha venido.
Gran salto diera en los moros;
en Montes-d'Oca, el castillo,
venciera todos los moros
y prendió los reyes cinco.) [5]

The following scene takes place in the palace where the strong-willed Prince Sancho is receiving a lesson in swordplay. He remarks that according to his horoscope he will be killed by a hurled weapon, and that the one responsible for his death will be closely related to him. The entrance of Urraca who has been hunting and is carrying a bloody javelin leads him to believe that she must be the person referred to in the horoscope, and he makes threats against her. The Moorish king whom Rodrigo had captured presents himself to King Fernando and tells how Rodrigo had captured him along with three other kings in a battle between five hundred Castilians and six thousand Moors. When Rodrigo arrives, he is called "Mió Cide" by the Moorish king, who explains that the title means "My Lord." Fernando decrees that Rodrigo shall be called "El Cid" from then on. [6]

Jimena, dressed in mourning, accompanied by squires who are also dressed in mourning, enters in order to lodge a protest with King Fernando:

Castro	Ballad
FIRST SQUIRE	
The king is seated in his high-backed chair.	The king is seated in his high-backed chair, settling disagree-ments among his unruly subjects.
JIMENA	
For me to throw myself at his feet, what does it matter that he be seated? If he is great, if he is just, let him reward the good and punish the bad; for punishment	Generous and just, he rewards the good and punishes the bad; for punishment and rewards develop faithful vassals. Trailing long mourning garments thirty noble-

and rewards develop faithful vassals.

DIEGO LAÍNEZ

Trailing long robes of mourning the squires of Count Lozano's daughter Jimena entered four by four. All look at her attentively, the palace becomes quiet, and in order to make her complaint she kneels at the dais.

JIMENA

Sire, three months ago today my father died at the hands of a youngster whom your hands brought up to be a murderer. Don Rodrigo de Vivar, haughty, proud and unruly, profaned your righteous laws, and you proudly protect him. Your eyes are his informers, in your seclusion he finds sanctuary, in your favor he finds freedom which results in harm for me. If just kings represent God's semblance and charge on the earth for humble humans, one who discourages justice and encourages wrongdoing should not be a well-feared and well-loved king. Let those who do evil not be protected by your justice which is the tree of our protection, for they are unworthy of even seeing its branches. Your eyes and your feeling deceive you, and forgive me if I speak disrespectfully, for by word of mouth a woman may disclose an affront. . . .

RODRIGO (*aside*)

My heart would give you blood in want of tears, my beloved.

JIMENA (*aside*)

Alas, Rodrigo! Alas, honor! Alas, my dear; where does a sense of duty lead you?

men entered, the squires of Jimena, Count Lozano's daughter. The mace bearers being dismissed, the palace was in suspense, and thus she began her complaints, kneeling before the dais:—Sire, it has been six months today since my father died at the hands of a youngster whom your hands brought up to be a murderer. Four times I have come to your feet, and each time I received promises; never did I receive justice. Don Rodrigo de Vivar, a proud and vain stripling, profanes your just laws, and you uphold the transgressor; you watch over and conceal him, and after he is in a safe place you punish your magistrates because they cannot seize him. If just kings represent God's semblance and charge on the earth for humble humans, one who fails in justice and encourages wrongdoing should not be a well-feared and well-loved king. Your eyes and your feeling deceive you! Forgive me if I speak disrespectfully to you, for a wrong done to a woman turns respect into an affront.—Let there be no more, noble lady, replied Fernando the First, because your complaints would soften a heart of steel and marble. If I do protect don Rodrigo, I protect him for your own good; the time will come when because of him you will change your tears into joy.

KING

Let there be no more, Jimena; let
that be enough! Arise, and do not
weep so, for your complaints
would soften a heart of steel and
marble. And it may be that some
day you will change your tears
into joy, and if I have protected
Rodrigo, perhaps I protect him
for you.

ESC. 1.º

(Sentado está el señor Rey en su
silla de respaldo.

JIMENA

Para arrojarme a sus pies ¿qué
importa que esté sentado? Si es
magno, si es justiciero, premie al
bueno y pene al malo, que casti-
gos y mercedes hacen seguros
vasallos.

DIEGO

Arrastrando luengos lutos, en-
traron de cuatro en cuatro escu-
deros de Jimena, hija del conde
Lozano. Todos atentos la miran,
suspenso quedó palacio, y para
decir sus quejas se arrodilla en los
estrados.

JIMENA

Señor, hoy hace tres meses que
murió mi padre a manos de un
rapaz, a quien las tuyas para
matador criaron. Don Rodrigo de
Vivar, soberbio, orgulloso y bravo,
profanó tus leyes justas, y tú le
amparas ufano. Son tus ojos sus
espías, tu retrete su sagrado, tu
favor sus alas libres, y su libertad
mi daño. Si de Dios los reyes
justos la semejanza y el cargo
representan en la tierra con los
humildes humanos, no debiera de
ser rey bien temido y bien amado,

(Sentado está el señor Rey en su
silla de respaldo, de su gente mal
regida desavenencias juzgando.
Dadivoso y justiciero premia al
bueno y pena al malo; que casti-
gos y mercedes hacen seguros
vasallos. Arrastrando luengos lutos
entraron treinta fidalgos escuderos
de Jimena, fija del conde Lozano.
Despachados los maceros quedó
suspenso el palacio, y así comenzó
sus quejas humillada en los estra-
dos:—Señor, hoy hace seis meses
que murió mi padre a manos de
un muchacho, que las tuyas para
matador criaron. Cuatro veces he
venido a tus pies, y todas cuatro
alcancé prometimientos, justicia
jamás alcanzo. Don Rodrigo de
Vivar, rapaz orgulloso y vano, pro-
fana tus justas leyes, y tú amparas
un profano: Tú le celas, tú le en-
cubres, y después de puesto en
salvo castigas a tus merinos, por-
que no pueden prendallo. Si de
Dios los buenos reyes la semejanza
y el cargo representan en la tierra
con los humildes humanos, no de-
biera de ser rey bien temido y
bien amado, quien fallesce en la
justicia y esfuerza los desacatos.
¡Mal lo miras! mal lo piensas! Per-

quien desmaya la justicia y es-
fuerza los desacatos. A tu justicia,
señor, que es árbol de nuestro
amparo, no se arrimen los mal-
hechores, indignos de ver sus
ramos. Mal lo miras, mal lo sien-
tes, y perdona si mal hablo; que
en boca de una mujer tiene licen-
cia un agravio. . . .

RODRIGO (*aparte*)
Sangre os dieran mis entrañas
para llorar, ojos claros.

JIMENA (*aparte*)
¡Ay, Rodrigo! ¡Ay, honra! ¡Ay,
ojos! ¿Adónde os lleva el cuidado?

REY
No haya más, Jimena, baste.
Levantaos, no lloréis tanto, que
ablandaran vuestras quejas en-
trañas de acero y mármol; que
podrá ser que algún día troquéis
en placer el llanto; y si he guar-
dado a Rodrigo, quizá para vos
le guardo. . . .)

dona si mal te fablo, que la in-
juria en la mujer vuelve el respeto
en agravio.—No haya más, gentil
doncella, respondió el primer Fer-
nando, que ablandaran vuesas
quejas un pecho de acero y már-
mol. Si yo guardo a Don Rodrigo,
para vueso bien lo guardo; tiempo
vendrá que por él convirtáis en
gozo el llanto . . .)[7]

(II, 192a ff.).

Castro's direct borrowing from the ballad is very much in evidence here. But it is also evident that he did not hesitate to make
many changes in his adaptation. His technique in assigning parts
of the ballad to three different speakers instead of having one
character recite it in its entirety has been criticized by one editor
of the play: ". . . In his adaptation of the ballad to the first part
of the scene, Castro shows a notable lack of his usual skill in
handling his ballad sources, and the contradictions and incon-
sistencies can hardly be explained away. The ballad is clumsily
distributed among the various personages, and some of the lines
interpolated by the dramatist, lines 1715 and 1716 for example,
are quite inane."[8]

The king again banishes Rodrigo in order to placate Jimena.
But the friendly *abrazo* (embrace) which Fernando gives the
young man is proof that the latter has not lost favor with his mon-

arch. As the act comes to an end, Rodrigo and Jimena look at each other without speaking, but Jimena's aside speeches, "I persecute what I adore," and "adored enemy," indicate the conflict within her heart.

At the beginning of the third act, Urraca confesses to Arias Gonzalo that she is in love with Rodrigo, but she realizes that Rodrigo's interest is completely centered in Jimena. A suggestion by Arias Gonzalo that she accept a non-Castilian for her husband is rejected by the princess. When King Fernando enters, Urraca complains to him that she fears being left disinherited when he dies, in view of her brother Sancho's animosity toward her. The king promises that he will take steps to bequeath her an estate. Arias Gonzalo and Fernando then discuss the question of Calahorra, which is claimed by both Castile and Aragon, a question which will be decided by a duel between an armed champion from each kingdom. The king is annoyed by an announcement that the persistent Jimena requests an audience. She again demands satisfaction against Rodrigo:

Castro	Ballad
When each day dawns I see the one who killed my father, mounted on his horse with a sparrow hawk in his hand. To my country home where I mitigate my sorrow he comes impertinent, free and inconsiderate; he looks, listens, goes and comes and in order to spite me he shoots arrows into the wind against my dovecote, arrows which strike me in the heart. He kills my little doves, even those which are still in brood. The blood which they shed has spattered my silken skirt. I sent word to him to desist, he answered by threatening me, which will leave lifeless a body that has no soul. A king who does not do justice should no longer reign, nor should he go about on horseback nor dally with the queen.	. . . I live under a cloud of shame, Sire, my mother died because of it; when each day dawns I see the one who killed my father, mounted on his horse with a sparrow hawk in his hand. In order to spite me more, he lets it feed in my dovecote, and thus kills my little doves, even those which are still in brood. The blood which they shed has stained my silken skirt. I sent word to him to desist, he answered by threatening me. A king who does not do justice should no longer reign, nor should he go about on horseback nor have parlance with the queen. . . .

(*Cada día que amanece, veo
quien mató a mi padre, caballero
en un caballo, y en su mano un
gavilán; a mi casa de placer,
donde alivio mi pesar, curioso,
libre y ligero, mira, escucha, viene
y va, y por hacerme despecho dis-
para a mi palomar flechas, que a
los vientos tira, y en el corazón me
dan; mátame mis palomicas, criadas y por criar; la sangre que sale
de ellas me ha salpicado el brial;
enviéselo a decir, envióme a
amenazar con que ha de dejar sin
vida cuerpo que sin alma está.
Rey que no hace justicia ni debría
de reinar, ni pasear en caballo, ni
con la Reina folgar.*)
　　　　(II, 195b ff.).

(—*Con mancilla vivo, Rey, con
ella murió mi madre; cada día que
amanece veo al que mató a mi
padre, caballero en un caballo, y
en su mano un gavilane; por
facerme más despecho cébalo en
mi palomare, mátame mis palo-
millas criadas y por criare; la
sangre que sale d'ellas teñido me
ha mi briale: enviéselo a decire,
envióme a amenazare. Rey que no
face justicia non debiera de rei-
nare, ni cabalgar en caballo, ni
con la reina fablare, . . .*)[9]

The king, suspecting that Jimena is in love with Rodrigo, has a servant announce the false news that he has met death at the hands of the Moors. Jimena nearly faints. Piqued when she learns that she has been deceived, she rashly promises that she will marry any nobleman who brings her Rodrigo's head. If a non-noble does the deed, he will receive half of her wealth.

The Cid, who is on a pilgrimage to Santiago, is depicted as an ideal Christian knight who says grace before each meal and who abhors such unseemly and non-Christian conduct as gluttony, impiety, and loose-mouthed talk. While he earnestly tells his followers that there are many roads to Heaven no matter what one's status in life may be, plaintive pleas are heard from a loathsome leper who has fallen into a quagmire. Although his companions turn away, the Cid helps the leper to his feet, kisses his hand, covers him with his cloak, and the two eat from the same plate. For the first part of this scene, Castro follows to a certain extent Durán's ballad No. 742 or one very much like it. After the Cid shows great compassion toward the leper, that night when Rodrigo is asleep, the leper awakens him by breathing upon his shoulders, and soon identifies himself as St. Lazarus. He predicts a future of great promise for Rodrigo:

Castro

I am Saint Lazarus, Rodrigo! I
was the poor man whom you
honored; and so much is God
pleased by what you did for me,
that you will be a prodigy famous
in our time, a miracle-working
captain, an invincible conqueror,
so much so that you are the only
one whom human beings will see
gain victory after death. And as
proof that this is so, whenever you
become aware of that vapor, that
divine breath that forcibly sends
the feeling of warmth to your
heart, undertake any deed, ask for
glory of any kind, for the Patron
Saint of Spain promises you victory.

(*San Lázaro soy, Rodrigo; yo fui
el pobre a quien honraste, y tanto
a Dios agradaste con lo que hiciste
conmigo, que serás un imposible
en nuestros siglos, famoso, un cap-
itán milagroso, un vencedor in-
vencible; y tanto, que sólo a ti
los humanos te han de ver después
de muerto vencer. Y en prueba de
que es así, en sintiendo aquel
vapor, aquel soberano aliento que
por la espalda violento te pasa al
pecho el calor, emprende cualquier hazaña, solicita cualquier
gloria, pues te ofrece la victoria el
Santo Patrón de España; . . .*)
(II, 200a)

Ballad

I am Saint Lazarus, Rodrigo, I
who have come to talk to you. I
am the leper to whom you did so
much good for the love of God.
Rodrigo, God loves you well, and
has granted you that whatever
you undertake in battle or other
affairs, you will carry out to your
honor, which will each day be
greater. You will be feared by all,
by Christians as well as Moors,
and your enemies will not be able
to do you harm. You will die an
honored death, and never having
been defeated, you will still be
victorious. God sends you his
blessing.

(—*San Lázaro soy, Rodrigo, yo,
que a te hablar venía; yo soy el
gafo a que tú por Dios tanto bien
hacías. Rodrigo, Dios bien te
quiere, otorgado te tenía que lo
que tú comenzares en lides, o en
otra guisa, lo cumplirás a tu honra
y crecerá cada día. De todos serás
temido, de cristianos y morisma,
y que los tus enemigos empecerte
no podrían. Morirás tú muerte
honrada, no tu persona vencida,
tú serás el vencedor, Dios su ben-
dición te envía. . . .*)[10]

In the play, St. Lazarus ends his discourse by telling the Cid
that his king has need of him. The king is indeed troubled, for he
fears that there is no Castilian knight who will be able to defeat
the seemingly invincible Aragonese champion Martín González in
a duel which will decide whether Calahorra will belong to Castile
or to Aragon. While the king is discussing the matter with some

close advisers, Martín González and the Cid arrive at the conference at the same time. The overbearing Aragonese champion heaps insults upon the Castilians and belittles Rodrigo when the latter says that he will uphold the honor of Castile. As Martín González leaves, he boasts that he will deliver Calahorra to his king and Rodrigo's head to Jimena.

Jimena, at home, admits to her maid Elvira that she committed a grave error when she promised to marry any nobleman who would bring her the head of Rodrigo. She expresses the fear that Martín González will be victor in the duel. To add to her sorrow, she receives a letter from don Martín in which he tells her to cast aside her mourning garb and to put on a wedding dress, promising to bring her Rodrigo's head as he leaves to avenge Count Lozano. Jimena blindly makes her way to her room and cries out that she adores the image of her enemy, Rodrigo, whom she is sending to his death and for whom she weeps.

The scene is again in the palace. King Fernando, perturbed over the unfriendly and arrogant way in which Prince Sancho treats his younger brothers and sisters, informs him of his plans to bequeath to each of his children part of the territory over which he rules. Sancho vows that as soon as his father dies he will seize control of all the lands which the others inherit, claiming that they are rightfully his by virtue of his being the oldest son. The king voices the hope that his maledictions may fall on Sancho if he fails to obey his commands. The unpredictable Jimena, dressed in finery instead of mourning, enters, and although her heart is full of sorrow she tries to give the impression that the letter which she received from Martín González has filled her heart with joy. A messenger announces that an Aragonese gentleman (or a gentleman from Aragon) has arrived, who is bringing Rodrigo's head to Jimena. All present believe that the Cid has been killed in the duel. Jimena, overcome with grief, tells of her love for Rodrigo, whom the laws of honor forced her to persecute. All are greatly relieved when Rodrigo enters, saying that he has come to present his head to Jimena, who had not specified whether it should be the head of a live man or of a dead man. The head of don Martín is outside hanging on the Cid's spear. Rodrigo asks that Jimena become his wife, which she and the king approve. The betrothal will take place that evening, and the plays ends.[11]

A student of literature can never feel absolutely certain that his

interpretation of a work of a bygone age represents what the author had in mind. This feeling of uncertainty is compounded
when a present-day English-speaking reader tries to interpret dramatic literature of Spain's Golden Age (1550–1681) with its stress
on the code of honor, orthodox Catholicism, and the divine right
of kings.[12] A similar feeling of uncertainty arises when one tries to
appreciate or evaluate a Golden Age play in the light of present-
day attitudes. The behavior of Jimena and Rodrigo in the play
which has just been discussed is an excellent case in point. To the
modern reader, many of Jimena's actions seem nonsensical, ab-
surd, and incredible, because the reader cannot accept with equa-
nimity her insistence upon persecuting Rodrigo and seeking his
death while at the same time she admits and confesses her profound love for him. When one bears in mind that Count Lozano
in a fit of anger slapped the face of the elderly and decrepit Diego
Laínez, thus depriving him of his priceless "honor," and that he
refused to consider offering an apology, and that he used insulting
words toward Rodrigo, thus helping to bring about his own death,
one can only say that, from our point of view, "He asked for it"
and "He had it coming to him." Jimena's reactions are all the more
difficult for us to understand when we know that her father was
killed, not in an underhanded or cowardly fashion, but by a single
opponent in a fair fight. Rodrigo's acquiescence to Jimena's perse-
cution of him and his willingness to suffer death in order to placate her for the loss of her father are likewise actions which the
modern reader takes with a grain of salt.

But in the eyes of many, although not all Spaniards of those
days, there was no other course of action for either Jimena or
Rodrigo. Caught in the web of the honor code which controlled
and directed the lives of the nobility, what the two protagonists
did was generally accepted as entirely commendable and natural.
The present writer's Chapter 4 makes clear how the code decreed
that it was Jimena's duty to at least try to avenge the death of her
father, and had she not made the attempt she would have lost
caste. Rodrigo, torn between his love for Jimena and his duty to
restore his father's honor, could act only as he did. His failure to
do so would have made him unworthy of Jimena. A present-day
critic of Spanish literature, commenting upon the real tragedy in
which Rodrigo and Jimena find themselves, and the unavoidable
path which they must follow, states that the heroism of Jimena

consists of her willingness to sacrifice; the grandeur of Rodrigo consists of his submission.[13]

II   *Le Cid of Pierre Corneille*

For a few decades in the sixteenth and seventeenth centuries, Spain was a world power, and Spanish influence was deep and widespread in much of western Europe. This was especially the case in France. "Spain was now present everywhere in custom and costume. . . . Spain was all-fashionable in the court and society where ruled the Spanish princess Anne of Austria. All people of education knew Spanish, and all the writers of plays, as we have seen, drew from the drama of Spain." [14] Two plays by the French dramatist Pierre Corneille (1606–1684), *Le Menteur* (*The Prevaricator*) and *Le Cid*, were based on works of Spanish dramatists of the Golden Age. The first of these plays, which derives from Juan Ruiz de Alarcón's *La verdad sospechosa* (*Suspicious Truth*), was the greatest comedy yet written in France. Corneille's indebtedness to Castro for *Le Cid*, one of the really great plays of French literature, has already been mentioned.

Le Cid, which was first presented late in 1636 or early in 1637, was an immediate success, and has attracted theatergoers from the seventeenth century on, as is attested by the fact that between 1680 and 1963 the play was performed 1,425 times at the Comédie-Française alone.[15]

The scene of *Le Cid* is Seville and the action begins in the morning. Chimène (Jimena) and Princess Urraque (Urraca) are in love with Rodrigue (Rodrigo). King Fernand (Fernando) has appointed don Diegue (Diego Laínez), Rodrigue's father, to be the preceptor of the young Prince, his son, an honor which don Gomes (el Conde Lozano) has greatly coveted. The two noblemen argue over the appointment until don Gomes, in a fit of anger, administers a buffet to the face of don Diegue. The latter, realizing that he is too old to avenge the affront, tells his son Rodrigue of the loss of his honor. The young man, torn between duty to his father and his love for Chimène, decides that his duty to his father must come first. He challenges the count to a duel and kills him. Chimène, torn between two powerful forces—a desire to gain revenge for the death of her father and her love for Rodrigue—demands justice against the young man who has killed her father. The king promises that justice will be done.

The Moors, planning to attack Seville during the night, have sent ten vessels up the Guadalquivir river. Don Diegue has assembled a force of five hundred friends, and Rodrigue leads them into a battle in which he gains a great victory and captures two Moorish kings. King Fernand decrees that since the Moorish kings have called Rodrigue "Cid," he will bear that title from then on.

Chimène appears once more before King Fernand to demand justice. She receives the false news that Rodrigue has lost his life in the battle and is greatly affected, but when she learns that she has been deceived, she rashly promises that she will marry any nobleman who brings her the head of Rodrigue. In such a case, according to the law of the land, a duel must take place between Rodrigue and a champion who supports the cause of Chimène. Don Sanche (not Prince Sancho) is accepted by Chimène as her champion. Rodrigue defeats don Sanche and in a magnanimous gesture has him deliver his sword to Chimène. The latter, believing that Rodrigue had been killed by don Sanche, sorrowfully confesses that she loved Rodrigue and asks the king to allow her to spend the rest of her life in a convent where she can weep incessantly over the loss of both her father and her lover. Great is her relief to learn that Rodrigue has not died. King Fernand orders that the two lovers will marry at the end of a year.

III The Two Cid Plays Compared

A comparison of Guillén de Castro's Cid I and Corneille's Le Cid shows that, in addition to the change from the three acts of the Spanish play to the five of Corneille's work, the verse forms used in each have nothing in common. In Castro's play one finds six different types of versification, namely redondilla, quintilla, décima and romance, all of these Spanish types, and also the Italianate canción and tercetos. In all, the type of strophe used varies at twenty-one places in the play. Le Cid is written chiefly in rhymed couplets of Alexandrine verses, each of which consists of from twelve to fourteen syllables, divided into hemistichs, with the stress generally on the sixth and twelfth syllables. The first two lines of Le Cid illustrate this type of verse:

> Elvire, m'as-tu fait un rapport bien sincère?
> Ne déguises-tu rien de ce qu'a dit mon père.

(Elvira, have you given me a real candid report?
Don't hold back anything that my father has said.)

Occasionally there are passages in which Corneille substitutes shorter lines of varying length for some of the Alexandrines. These passages follow no definite pattern of rhyme.

Corneille has also made several other changes in and deletions from his Spanish model. The scene of the French play is not Castile but Seville, a city which was not captured from the Moors until 1248, more than one hundred years after the death of the Cid. The following characters in Castro's work do not appear in *Le Cid:* the queen; Prince Sancho; Peransules; the two brothers of Rodrigo; the fencing master; Martín González; the shepherd; four Moors; the leper; one or two pages, and the supernumeraries.

Several incidents in the Spanish play are not found in the French tragedy. Among these incidents are the knighting of Rodrigo; the testing of the mettle of his three sons by Diego Laínez; Rodrigo's fight with the followers of the slain count and Urraca's orders that he be not harmed; Rodrigo's meeting with Urraca at the country home of the queen; his engagements in Castile with the Moors as described by the shepherd; Urraca's entrance in the second act bearing a bloody javelin; the banishment of Rodrigo to placate Jimena; his encounter with the leper; the dispute of Castile and Aragon over the possession of Calahorra with the subsequent duel between Rodrigo and Martín González; King Fernando's dividing of his kingdom among his five children and the triumphant return of the Cid from Aragon.

Many of these omissions are due to the fact that Corneille was limited by the conventions of the French theatre of his day, especially the unities of time and place. Thus the action in *Le Cid* is limited to twenty-four hours instead of the more than three years in which the action of the Spanish play takes place. Corneille's contemporaries pointed out that the hero has to compress three years of action into twenty-four hours and has to work through the night in order to do so. These twenty-four hours have been called "probably the most crowded day in all recorded time." In following the unity of place Corneille limited the action to the royal palace and its adjacency, but not to one room which strict observance of this unity would have required.

Other omissions were dictated by the type of audience for which Corneille wrote. A Spanish audience, familiar with the ballads that are the basis of Castro's play, and imbued with a deep religious fervor, could easily accept the bloodthirsty and barbaric scenes and the exaltation of the Cid as an ideal Christian knight which is exemplified by his encounter with the leper and his compassion toward that social outcast. But to a sophisticated theatrical audience of seventeenth-century Paris, the Cid's action in eating from the same plate with the leper and his offer to share his bed with him would have seemed ludicrous and would undoubtedly have provoked much criticism. Moreover, the conventions of the French theatre of that day did not permit such socially unacceptable characters as a leper to appear in a tragedy.

According to one critic of the French Classical drama, of the twenty-nine scenes in Le Cid, fourteen are entirely original, or nearly so. The other fifteen, including most of the important ones, follow the Spanish play closely, although one does find many variations from it.[16] A Spanish literary critic, Víctor Said Armesto, credits Corneille with much less originality than does Lancaster. Said Armesto asserts that Corneille translated Castro's Cid I.[17] An unbiased reader of the two works will agree that Said Armesto's assertion is inaccurate because Corneille did not really translate Castro's work. But one can find in Le Cid lines which are reminiscent of lines in Las mocedades del Cid. Typical examples are the following: Diego Laínez says to Rodrigo, ". . . this blemish on my honor, which extends to yours also, wash it away with blood, for only blood removes such stains" (. . . esta mancha de mi honor / que al tuyo se extiende, lava / con sangre; que sangre sola / quita semejantes manchas" II, 176a). Don Diegue says to Rodrigue, "It is only in blood that one washes away such an affront" (Ce n'est que dans le sang qu'on lave un tel outrage"), I, line 274. In a later scene, Jimena tells Elvira, ". . . for half of my life has killed the other half" (. . . que la mitad de mi vida / ha muerto la otra mitad"), II, 184a). Chimène tells Elvire, "Half of my life has placed the other half in the tomb" (La moitié de ma vie a mis l'autre au tombeau"), III, line 800.

The great and immediate popularity of Le Cid aroused the jealousy of certain French writers who considered themselves to be the leading dramatists of the day. These rivals of Corneille brought such charges as the following against the play and its author: *Le Cid* was a translation of Castro's work; Chimène's willingness to marry the man who had killed her father was improbable and shocking; too much action was crowded into twenty-four hours. This dispute, "The Quarrel of the Cid," is a very interesting chapter of French literary history, but its details are not pertinent to this work. Those who are interested in reading more about it may consult any reliable history of French literature.

A minor and less vituperative "Quarrel of the Cid" has been waged until the present day by commentators upon *Las mocedades del Cid* and *Le Cid*. The judgments issued upon each work seem to depend in part upon the national origin of each commentator. Ernest Martinenche, for example, like most French critics, recognizes Corneille's great debt to Guillén de Castro, asserting that, except for the second interview between Rodrigue and Chimène, there is not a scene which Corneille has not borrowed from the Spanish dramatist. But he goes on to say, "And yet, what an abyss separates the Spanish tableau and the French drama . . . to prune [as Corneille has pruned Castro's work] is veritably to create." [18] A. Morel Fatio, in discussing French imitation of Spanish works in the seventeenth century, calls it "intelligent imitation which is able to create works more beautiful, more perfect than the originals," referring to Corneille's *Le Cid* and *Le Menteur*.[19]

Spanish critics, on the other hand, refuse in general to admit that Corneille's play is superior to Castro's.[20] One of our compatriots, who wrote the first history of Spanish literature to appear in any language, makes the following statement: "Nor has he [Corneille] shown in his exhibition more spirit or power than his Spanish predecessor. Indeed, sometimes he has fallen into considerable errors, which are wholly his own." [21] Two of these errors, according to Ticknor, are the unity of time and the transfer of the setting of the play to Seville. In the opinion of an eminent British Hispanist of the Old School, "Corneille took over the situation and created a masterpiece which completely overshadowed Castro's play. The names of other dramatists who treated the same theme are very properly forgotten; another great dramatization of the Cid story is about as likely as another great dramatization of the story of Romeo and Juliet." [22] Quotations which refer to this minor and nonvituperative "Quarrel of the Cid" could go on at great length, and perhaps no more fitting climax to it can be given than the statement that "Castro, if unable to produce a masterpiece, at least inspired one." [23]

IV   *Las mocedades del Cid* (*Comedia Segunda*)
(*The Youthful Deeds of the Cid—Cid II*)

Castro begins his play after the death of King Fernando. San-cho, now King of Castile, embarks upon military expeditions to deprive his brothers and sisters of the territory which their father had bequeathed them. His brother García, King of Galicia, and his sister Elvira were his first victims. Sancho next takes steps to defeat his older brother, Alonso (later King Alfonso), who had inherited the kingdom of Leon. The play begins with the struggle between these two brothers in a battle scene in which victory seems to favor one side and then the other. The Cid, who comes to the aid of Sancho, swings the tide of battle and liberates his king who had been captured by the forces of Alonso. When Sancho orders his men to pursue Alonso and his troops, the Cid provokes his anger by suggesting that such action is unworthy of a Christian. Rodrigo then reminds him of the deathbed scene in which King Fernando, surrounded by his children, hears Urraca bitterly reproach him for having neglected to provide territory for her to rule. The king, remembering that Zamora has not been be-queathed to any of his children, tells Urraca that the city is hers, adding "May my curse fall upon anyone who should ever take it from you." Only Sancho keeps silence as the others say, "So be it." This scene is based on the ballad, *Morir vos queredes, padre, / Sant Miguel vos haya el alma* . . . ("So you are ready to die, my father, may St. Michael receive your soul . . .").[24]

Sancho leads his troops against Zamora in order to wrest control of the city from his sister Urraca. Greatly perturbed as the appari-tion of his father, carrying a bloody javelin, comes forth from the earth, he orders his men to withdraw, but he does not abandon the siege. Meanwhile, Bellido Dolfos, a resident of Zamora, re-ceives permission from Urraca to embark upon a plan to free the city from the siege at the cost of the life of one person whom he does not name. Purposely arousing the antagonism of Arias Gon-zalo and his five sons, Bellido Dolfos is forced to flee from Za-mora. He seeks refuge in the encampment of King Sancho, to whom he vows fealty and promises to show him how he can capture the beleaguered city. Just then the voice of Arias Gonzalo is heard as he shouts a warning to King Sancho from the walls of Zamora in the well-known ballad, *Rey don Sancho, rey don Sancho, / no digas que no te aviso, . . .* ("King don Sancho, King don Sancho, do not say that I have not warned you, . . .").[25] The import of the warning is that Bellido, a murderer and traitor, should not be trusted.

The Cid, who is acquainted with the traitor's background, tries to persuade the king to imprison him or kill him, but to no avail. As Rodrigo becomes more and more vehement, he incurs the wrath of Sancho, who banishes him for one year. The Cid retorts: "You banish me for one year, I banish myself for four." [26] Sancho soon realizes that he erred in banishing Rodrigo and has him called back to the encampment, a request which the Cid obeys as a loyal vassal. But the king, in his eagerness to learn how he can capture Zamora, fails to heed the warnings which he has just heard, and leaves his encampment accompanied by Bellido Dolfos. When an opportune moment arrives, Bellido uses the king's own spear to wound him mortally and then flees toward Zamora, pursued by Rodrigo, who fails to overtake him. As Rodrigo stands before the walls of Zamora, he is bitterly rebuked by Urraca, who accuses him of being arrogant, ungrateful, and injudicious for having rejected marriage with her in order to marry the daughter of a vassal.[27]

The mortally wounded King Sancho, with the spear protruding from his chest, is carried onto the stage by Diego Ordóñez de Lara. Sancho confesses that he has been punished justly for his disobedience. Then, after asking forgiveness of his brothers and sisters, and forgiving Bellido Dolfos, he dies. In this scene Guillén de Castro paraphrases part of ballad 785 in Durán's collection: *Después que Bellido D'Olfos / aquel traidor afamado . . .* ("After Bellido D'Olfos, that well-known traitor . . .").

Bellido Dolfos, fleeing from the Cid, has gained entrance to Zamora, but he is imprisoned when Urraca learns of the assassination of her brother. The funeral procession of King Sancho is now viewed from the walls of Zamora. His soldiers, garbed in mourning, pass by silently, four abreast, sword in hand, followed by the outstanding noblemen of Castile who carry the bier. The king's body is seen, covered with blood, the spear protruding from his chest, his crown lying at his feet. As soon as the procession has passed, a mounted knight from the royal encampment rides up to the walls of Zamora. It is Diego Ordóñez de Lara, armed, garbed in mourning, with a shroud over his shoulder and a crucifix in his right hand. Accusing the inhabitants of Zamora of complicity in the death of King Sancho, he issues his famous *reto*. A *reto* is a curse as well as a challenge, and in his *reto* Diego Ordóñez curses the inhabitants of Zamora of all ages, the dead along with the living and even those unborn. He curses streets, buildings, bread, meat, water, and wine. According to medieval law, the one who issues a *reto* must meet five champions from the accused city on the field of combat. Moreover, he must defeat them one by one without leaving the lists.[28]

Arias Gonzalo, in a chiding tone of voice, asks Diego Ordóñez de Lara why children are to blame for what adults have done and how can lifeless things be included in his *reto*. He then reminds him of the responsibilties which he has incurred by his action. Diego Ordóñez replies that he will uphold his charge at dawn on the following day.[29]

The next few scenes of the play take place in Toledo. Sancho's brother Alonso, whose forces had been routed at the beginning of the play, has found refuge in the court of Alimaimón, the Moorish king of that city. Alonso falls in love with Zaida, the beautiful daughter of the King of Sevilla and niece of Alimaimón. Zaida reciprocates the attentions of Alonso. One afternoon, as Alonso and Zaida speak in the garden of their mutual love, Alimaimón and two Moorish hermits enter. Alonso, in order not to disclose his interest in Zaida, pretends to have fallen asleep under a myrtle shrub. The hermits, unaware of the presence of Alonso, tell Alimaimón of a prophecy regarding the future of Toledo. According to this prophecy, the city, despite its impregnable position, will be forced to surrender some day after a long siege prevents food from being brought in. When they see Alonso lying in the shade, they realize that if he has heard them, they have disclosed an important secret of state. The hermits urge Alimaimón to kill Alonso, but the king hesitates to use violence on one whom he has promised to protect. One of the hermits then suggests that they ascertain whether the soil under Alonso's mouth is moist, for if it is so, that is proof that he is in a profound sleep. The astute Alonso, aware of his danger, takes measures to moisten the soil. Southey's account of this scene, which apparently has not been preserved in ballad form, follows:

"And they said to him [Alimaymon], would you know whether or not he sleepeth? and he answered, Yea: and they say, Go then and wake him, and if he have drivelled he hath slept, but if not he hath been awake and hath heard us. Then King Don Alonso immediately wetted the pillow and feigned himself hard to be awakened, so that Alimaymon thought he slept." [30]

Castro's version is based on parts of the ballad, *En Toledo estaba Alfonso, / hijo del rey don Fernando:* . . . ("Alfonso, son of King Fernando, was in Toledo: . . .").[31] Alfonso, feigning sleep, hears a Moor suggest to Alimaimón that he kill the Christian. Alfonso's hair rises through fear, and Alimaimón presses it down with his hand, but when the king removes his hand the hair immediately rises. Persuaded that this means that Alfonso will eventually be king of the city, Alimaimón draws his sword in order to kill him, but Zaida intervenes and saves the life of her lover. Shortly after this incident, Peransules arrives with the news of Sancho's death, which means that Alfonso should leave at once for Castile. Zaida promises to go with him.

Meanwhile in Zamora, Arias Gonzalo and his sons prepare to uphold the fame of their city in the trial by combat with Diego Ordóñez. When Urraca hears that her revered counselor plans to be the first to enter the lists, she voices strong objection, reminding him that he had promised her father, King Fernando, on his deathbed never to forsake her. This scene is based on the ballad *¿Dónde vais, mi padre viejo, / o para qué estáis armado?* ("Where are you going, venerable father, and for what purpose are you armed?").[32] Much against his will Arias Gonzalo yields to Urraca's pleas and chooses his youngest son, Pedro Arias, to be the first to face the vengeful Diego Ordóñez, who has driven five stakes into the ground in order to keep count of his victims. The inexperienced youngster is no match for his opponent, who soon kills him. After pulling one stake from the ground and throwing it into the air, Diego Ordóñez taunts the father of his victim with the remark: "Don Arias, send forth another son, because this one has been accounted for." [33] The second son suffers the fate of his brother, which elicits another taunt from Diego Ordóñez: "Don Arias, send forth the third for the second has been dispatched." [34] As Arias Gonzalo sends his third son to the lists, he hopes to arouse his thirst for vengeance by suggesting that he take a close look at the innocent blood of his two brothers on the field and on the arm and sword of his opponent.[35]

A terrific struggle ensues, but Diego Ordóñez manages to deliver a mortal blow to Rodrigo Arias, the third son of Arias Gonzalo. Rodrigo Arias, striking out in desperation, cuts the reins of the horse of his adversary and severely injures the animal, which carries its rider out of the enclosure before he can dismount. The dying son of Arias Gonzalo stays within. The question of Zamora's guilt or innocence is now one for the judges to decide: ". . . The judges now come forth and order him [Diego Ordóñez] to leave, for they will decide the case according to the laws of Spain." [36]

The decision of the judges is that Zamora is not guilty of treason and that Diego Ordóñez is the victor in the trial by combat. Bellido Dolfos has been sentenced to be tied to four horses and thus torn to pieces. The arrival of Alfonso and Zaida is announced. When Spaniards from many parts of the nation assemble, Alfonso asks them to swear allegiance to him. All do so except Rodrigo de Bivar, who cites as reason for his refusal the gossip of the lower classes which accuses him of being Alfonso's accomplice in having King Sancho assassinated. The Cid suggests that the gossip can be answered by having the king declare his innocence in a solemn oath. The king is angered but he agrees to do so, and Rodrigo is not afraid to administer the oath, which is read as Alfonso places his hand upon a bolt of iron and a wooden crossbow upon which there is a crucifix. In this famous oath the Cid expresses the wish that Alfonso may be slain treacherously by Asturian peasants who use base weapons if he was in any way involved in the death of his brother. The angry king swears that he is innocent and then banishes the Cid because of his lack of respect.[37] But the two are almost immediately reconciled. The king accepts the crown from Rodrigo's hand; Zaida, now a Christian, changes her name to María; Alfonso gives her his hand in marriage as the play ends.

V A Note on Castro's Ballad Technique

Castro's debt to the ballads is very much in evidence in the two *Cid* plays. Some of them he incorporated skillfully, either entirely or in part, with little if any change. But he was less successful in a few cases in which he distributed parts of a ballad among a few actors rather than having it recited or sung by one person. Specific examples are: Jimena's complaint to King Fernando (II, 192a); the warning of Arias Gonzalo to King Sancho (II, 222a); and the third engagement in the trial of combat of Diego Ordóñez de Lara after he has been carried out of the enclosure by his horse (II, 245b). Likely to be unnoticed by many readers are the numerous instances in which Castro incorporates only a line or two from some well-known ballad into his plays. Víctor Said Armesto calls attention to some of these in his edition of the two *Cid* plays. An additional instance which seems to have escaped notice is a line in *Cid II* in which Alonso tells Zaida: "Pledge or sell my villas" (*Empeña o vende mis villas*), II, 215a. This calls to mind the following lines spoken by Count Irlos as he prepares to leave France for a sojourn in Persia: "You may sell anyone of the villas and pledge any city you wish" (*Podéis vender cualquier villa / y empeñar cualquier ciudade*).[38] These two lines are found almost verbatim in Castro's *Count Irlos* (I, 382a).

CHAPTER 6

Rodrigo Díaz de Vivar, The Cid

I The Cid of History

RODRIGO (or Ruy) Díaz de Vivar was born toward the middle of the eleventh century, probably in the year 1043. Vivar (also spelled Bivar), which is generally considered to be his birthplace, is a village about four miles north of Burgos in Old Castile. His father, Diego Laínez, was a descendant of Laín Calvo, a famous Castilian judge of the ninth century. His mother was likewise of noble stock. Of Rodrigo's early years we know very little. After the death of his father about the year 1058, Rodrigo was reared in the court of King Fernando I, el Magno (the Great), at the side of Fernando's oldest son, Prince Sancho. Close ties developed between Rodrigo and the Prince, who conferred a great honor upon him by dubbing him knight.

Sancho succeeded to the throne of Castile in 1065 upon the death of his father, and continued to shower favors upon Rodrigo, appointing him to the rank of *alférez* (standard bearer), thus making him the most important among the officials of the royal court. The young standard bearer soon proved his mettle by defeating a champion of Navarre in a judicial hand-to-hand combat. This victory at the age of twenty-three gained great renown for him, and from then on he was called *campeador* (victor in battle). The young *campeador* also distinguished himself in several military expeditions of King Sancho, among them the siege of Zaragoza and the defeat of the forces of Sancho's brother Alfonso, who was banished from Castile and found sanctuary with the Moorish King of Toledo.

King Sancho, desiring to expand his sphere of influence, in 1072 besieged the city of Zamora which was under the control of his sister Urraca. In this famous siege, which is recounted in later epic material, ballads, and dramas, Rodrigo de Vivar gained renown for both bravery and military prowess. As the siege continued, the defenders of Zamora devised a bold stroke: "They sent forth a knight of great daring, called Vellido Adolfo, who made his way undetected into the camp of the besiegers, surprised the unexpectant King, and pierced his chest with his lance. This happened on Sunday, October 7, 1072." [1] This bold venture, which cost Sancho his life, should be remembered when one reads of its elaboration and distortion in the ballads as well as in Guillén de Castro's *Cid II* play.

After the death of Sancho, Alfonso returned to Zamora to take possession of the kingdom. The Castilians accused Urraca of complicity in the death of Sancho, and some even suspected that Alfonso had had a hand in the plot. The laws of those days decreed that upon the death by assassination of a ruler, his successor, if suspected of complicity in the deed, was bound to swear in a solemn oath that he was innocent of the accusation. According to tradition, the Cid alone of all the Castilian noblemen refused to kiss Alfonso's hand as a sign of allegiance unless the latter swore the prescribed oath before him. When Alfonso had sworn three times before the Cid that he had had no part in the death of Sancho, the Cid knelt to kiss the hand of the new King, but Alfonso angrily refused to allow him to do so. Menéndez Pidal calls this "poetic fiction," remarking that when Alfonso swore the oath, he was merely adhering to a customary juridical ritual and doing what was expected of him.[2]

Under Alfonso the Cid was no longer the highest ranking noble in the King's retinue as he had been under Sancho, for he was merely one among a large number of vassals. García Ordóñez, an implacable enemy of Rodrigo, replaced him as the king's standard bearer. But Alfonso did show favor toward the Cid by arranging in 1074 to have him marry Jimena Díaz, who was not only the niece of Alfonso, but also great-granddaughter of King Alfonso V of Leon. The issue of this marriage were a son, Diego, and two daughters, Cristina and María.

Toward the end of the year 1079 or early in 1080, the Cid went on a mission to Sevilla to collect the annual tribute which the Moorish King Motamid had agreed to pay Alfonso. While he was in Sevilla, the Cid intervened in a war between King Motamid and the King of Granada. The forces of the Cid defeated Motamid's enemies in a battle in which many prisoners were captured, one of whom was García Ordóñez. The Cid's resounding victory aroused considerable envy among the noblemen of the court, some of whom brought false accusations against him. The capture of García Ordóñez undoubtedly displeased Alfonso, who still rankled over the fact that Rodrigo had helped Sancho to defeat him. So it is not surprising that Alfonso, influenced by the continuing and implacable accusations against the Cid, banished him in 1081. Forced to leave Castile, Rodrigo, accompanied by a few loyal followers, joined forces with the Moorish King of Zaragoza in the latter's struggles against certain Moslem factions. On one occasion he fought at the side of Alfonso, who asked him to return to Castile, but the Cid preferred to remain in Zaragoza, over which he exercised a sort of protectorate, and where he stayed until 1087.

In the meantime, Alfonso had been waging war against the Moors of southern Spain. His success in these engagements led them to ask for aid of Yusuf, the Emir of Morocco. Yusuf landed in Spain with a large force in 1086 and not long after, he routed the Christian troops in a battle in which Alfonso was wounded. When Alfonso, faced with the danger of growing Moslem power, asked aid of Christendom, the Cid became reconciled with him and, in a series of forays, regained control of much of southern Spain for Alfonso, laying siege to Valencia, which he captured in 1089.

In the ten years which followed, the Cid was busily engaged in military expeditions, especially against Yusuf. He found himself in the curious situation of being reconciled with Alfonso on more than one occasion and then losing the favor of his truculent and suspicious monarch. He was sent into exile for the second time, his wife and his children were imprisoned, and his estates were ordered confiscated. His hold on Valencia during these years was precarious, but he did maintain control of the city until his death in 1099. He had the satisfaction of seeing his elder daughter, Cristina, married to Prince Ramiro of Navarre. His younger daughter, María, was married to Ramón Berenguer III, Count of Barcelona. His only son, Diego, died in battle in 1097. His wife, Jimena, probably aided by her son-in-law Count Ramón, managed to stay on in Valencia for a while after the death of Rodrigo, but the Christians were forced to abandon the city in 1102, taking with them the body of the Cid, which was given final burial in Castile.

II *The Cid of the Epic Poem*

Many scholars consider that the *Cantar de Mió Cid* (*Song of the Cid*) or *Poema del Cid* (*Poem of the Cid*) was written about 1140, some forty years after the death of the hero. E. R. Curtius, however, expresses the opinion that the Poem ". . . can hardly have been composed before 1180." [3] The original manuscript has been lost, but there is extant a copy of it made by a certain Pero Abad in 1307. This copy was not published until 1779, so it is clear that Guillén de Castro and other writers of his day were not influenced directly by that epic poem. But it did have an indirect influence upon them through its prosifications in the later chronicles, which in turn were the source of considerable ballad material. The poem consists of 3,730 lines, and it is divided into three *cantares* (songs): *Destierro del Cid* (*Banishment of the Cid*), *Cantar de las Bodas* (*Song of the Weddings*) and *La Afrenta de Corpes* (*The Affront of the Oak Grove of Corpes*).

Approximately the first fifty lines of the epic poem are missing, and there is another lacuna later in the poem. In his editions of this work, Menéndez Pidal fills in what is missing by quotations from the *Crónica de Veinte Reyes* (*Chronicle of Twenty Kings*). According to this chronicle, King Alfonso sent the Cid to southern Spain to collect the annual tribute from the Moorish Kings of Córdoba and Sevilla. While on this mission, he becomes involved in a war between Alfonso's vassal Almutamiz, King of Sevilla, and the King of Granada. Under the leadership of the Cid, the forces of Almutamiz are victorious in a battle in which many prisoners are captured, one of whom is the Castilian nobleman García Ordóñez. The Cid delivers the tribute which he has collected to King Alfonso, but soon jealous and envious courtiers are successful in arousing the king's anger against him, with the result that he receives written orders from the king to leave the kingdom within nine days.

As the epic poem begins, the Cid goes to Burgos accompanied by several of his followers who express a willingness to share exile with him. The terrified inhabitants of Burgos refuse to give him material aid. The Cid then hoodwinks two Jewish moneylenders, Raquel and Vidas, into lending him six hundred marks, giving them as security two chests filled with sand, which they are not to open until a year has passed. During his last night in Castile, the

Angel Gabriel appears to him in a dream. The next morning, after taking leave of his wife Jimena and his two small daughters, Elvira and Sol, whom he has left in the care of the monks of San Pedro de Cardeña, he leads his men into the territory of the Moorish King of Toledo. The Cid's forces capture two towns from the Moors and later rout the troops of the King of Valencia. In this battle they obtain immense booty, part of which Rodrigo sends as a gift to Alfonso. The king does not pardon him, but he does permit any of his subjects who wish to do so to join the Cid and his men. In another battle the Cid gains possession of his famous sword *Colada*. As Part I comes to an end, Rodrigo's men "are so rich that they cannot count their possessions" (Line 1086 of the Menéndez Pidal edition. See note 4 below).

In Part II, *The Song of the Weddings,* the Cid lays siege to Valencia, which surrenders after nine months. Rodrigo again sends presents to Alfonso, who permits Jimena and her two daughters to go to Valencia where they are reunited with the Cid. King Yusuf of Morocco brings a large army from Africa and besieges Valencia, but these Moslems are dealt a crushing defeat. The victors gain immense spoils, part of which is sent to Alfonso. Rodrigo's success in battle and his great wealth arouse the cupidity of two brothers, Diego and Fernando, *Infantes* (Counts) of Carrión, who ask King Alfonso to intercede on their behalf with the Cid so that they may marry his daughters. At a meeting on the banks of the Tagus River, the king gives a complete pardon to the Cid and asks him to grant permission for the marriage of his daughters to the counts. Rodrigo grudgingly accedes as he tells the king: "I place Elvira and Sol in your hands, give them to whomsoever you wish, for I am satisfied" (Lines 2088–89). The pointed remark "give them to whomsoever you wish," makes the king at least partly responsible should anything amiss develop. The counts accompany the Cid to Valencia where the ceremonies are held.

In Part III, *The Affront of the Oak Grove of Corpes,* the Cid's sons-in-law, Diego and Fernando, show cowardice when a lion escapes from its cage, and again in battle when King Búcar of Morocco attacks Valencia. The invaders from Africa are dispersed, the Cid kills Búcar and gains possession of another famous sword, *Tizón* or *Tizona* (Firebrand). The Counts of Carrión become the butts of numerous jests and are scorned because of their cowardice, all of which makes their stay in the Cid's household quite unpleasant. They ask and receive permission to take their wives to Carrión, but on the way, when they reach the Oak Grove of Corpes, they send their retinue ahead. Then they denude their wives and tie them to trees. After beating them unmercifully, they ride on, abandoning them to their fate. Feliz Muñoz, Cid's nephew, suspicious of the actions of the counts, follows at a distance, and rescues Elvira and Sol, whom he escorts to Valencia.

When Rodrigo demands justice of the king for the affront committed by his sons-in-law, Alfonso convokes Court in Toledo where he shows great honor to the Cid. The judgment of the Court is that the Counts of Carrión return to the Cid the swords *Colada* and *Tizona* which they had received as gifts. They are also ordered to repay the dowry of three thousand marks which the Cid had given them, and in addition they are to be subjected to a trial by combat. In this trial by combat, the counts and their friend Asur are defeated by three champions from the household of the Cid. Meanwhile, Elvira and Sol are espoused respectively to the Princes of Navarre and Aragon. The poem ends with the news of the death of Rodrigo de Vivar on the Feast of Pentecost. ". . . May he have Christ's forgiveness! May all of us both righteous and sinners likewise have it! This is the account of the Cid, the champion in battle; here ends the story" (Lines 3727–30).

The *Poema de Mió Cid*, which, as has been shown, was written not many years after the death of the hero, is closer chronologically to the events narrated than any other extant epic. It is the most realistic of all epic poems of any language or country, and provides considerable information about customs and laws of its day. Anyone who is interested in ascertaining just to what extent the poem does reflect historical personages and events should consult the introductions found in the edition of the poem by Menéndez Pidal. A few deviations from history deserve comment here. The historical daughters Cristina and María become Elvira and Sol in the epic poem, which makes no mention of Rodrigo's son Diego. The Counts of Carrión, Diego and Fernando, are historical characters, but there is no proof that they were married to the daughters of the Cid. There is likewise no historical basis for the hoodwinking of Raquel and Vidas, the moneylenders, nor for the episode of the escape of the lion and the cowardly comportment of the Cid's sons-in-law.[4] But all in all, the *Poema de Mió*

Cid does give us an unusually reliable account of life and historical characters in the last half of the eleventh century.

III   *The Cid of the Chronicles*

The compilers of the early chronicles accepted the epic poems as veridical sources and incorporated prose versions of them into their accounts. This is especially true of *La primera crónica general* (*The First General Chronicle*), which was begun in 1270 at the court of Alfonso the Learned [5] and in which one can find many passages presumably taken from the old epics. Thanks to these uncritical compilers of history, there has been preserved for posterity the essence of more than one lost epic poem. The part of *The First General Chronicle* which deals with the Cid during the reign of Alfonso VI corresponds fairly closely to the *Poem of the Cid*. It mentions among other episodes the banishment of the Cid, his deception of the moneylenders, his capture of Valencia, and his cowardly sons-in-law.

Neither history nor the epic poem tells us much about the Cid prior to the reign of Alfonso VI. *The First General Chronicle,* however, has references to the Cid during the earlier reigns of King Fernando the Great and King Sancho, many of which contravene what is historical. This is especially true of what happened when Alfonso fled to Toledo after his army had been defeated by Sancho's troops. From what can be gleaned from historical accounts, Alfonso spent his few months of exile in Toledo helping the king wage war against his Moorish enemies, or hunting bears and wild boars in the neighboring forests. When the news of the assassination of Sancho reached Toledo, the king gave Alfonso permission to return to Zamora.[6] The fictional and highly dramatic account in the *Chronicle* of what took place during Alfonso's stay in Toledo inspired many ballads, and through them became an important source of Guillén de Castro's *Cid II* play.

According to the *Chronicle,* one afternoon Alfonso was lying under a tree in the royal garden, feigning sleep, when he overheard King Mamún discuss with some advisers whether or not Toledo could be taken by force. The consensus was that the city could withstand a siege of eight years, after which it would be forced to surrender to the Christians. Later, as Alfonso and the king were walking about, they heard a Moor tell of a dream in which he saw Alfonso, mounted on a pig, enter Toledo to become lord of the city. On another occasion, Alfonso's hair mysteriously stood on end and the king was unable to make it lie flat in spite of his many efforts to do so. When he consulted his wise men about this troublesome incident, they replied that it foretold that Alfonso would become lord of Toledo. They suggested to the king that he kill Alfonso, which the king refused to do, requiring instead a promise from his royal guest that he be loyal to him and to his family.

During Alfonso's exile in Toledo, the inhabitants of Zamora vowed to remain loyal to their banished Leonese king, rather than swear fealty to the Castilianized King Sancho. In order to nip in the bud this show of resistance to his authority, Sancho had his troops lay siege to the city. It was during this siege that Vellido Adolfo (Vellido Dolfos) entered the Castilian camp and killed King Sancho with a spear. The *Chronicle* has expanded and embellished the incidents of this siege by including additional unhistorical material which was taken over by the ballads, and which is another important source for Castro's *Cid II* play. When Zamora was about to surrender, Vellido Dolfos, who is depicted as a cowardly conniving miscreant, told Urraca of a plan to keep the city from falling into Sancho's possession, and received from her a promise of great reward. His next step was to insult Arias Gonzalo, who, with his sons, drove him from the city. Fleeing to Sancho's camp, Vellido became his vassal and promised to show him a gate in Zamora which was never closed, through which he could lead his soldiers to capture the city. In spite of a solemn warning that Vellido was a traitor, which was directed to Sancho from the walls of Zamora, the king accompanied Vellido to see the gate, thereby meeting his doom when Vellido killed him with the royal spear. Pursued by Rodrigo de Vivar, the traitor fled to Zamora, where he was imprisoned.

Diego Ordóñez de Lara, accusing Zamora of complicity in the assassination, issued his famous *reto,* after which he met and killed three sons of Arias Gonzalo in the obligatory trial by combat. But since he had been carried out of the enclosure when his horse was wounded in the third encounter, the issue of Zamora's guilt would have to be decided by the judges. When Alfonso returned to Zamora from his exile in Toledo, the Cid refused to kiss his hand unless he made a public declaration of innocence in the

death of Sancho. The king did so, whereupon the Cid offered to
kiss the ruler's hand but was angrily rebuffed. The Cid was eventually forgiven by Alfonso and helped him in his wars against the
Moors.

The *Chronicle* continues with an account of Rodrigo's activities
from the time Alfonso sent him on the mission to collect tribute
from the Kings of Sevilla and Córdoba, which is the starting point
of the epic poem, and continues until his capture of Valencia. This
section of the *Chronicle* ends with the fanciful statement that St.
Peter appeared to the Cid in a vision, telling him that he would
die within thirty days, but assuring him that he would be victorious over King Búcar even after death. So when Búcar's forces
do attack Valencia, the body of the Cid is placed upon a horse and
led into battle array against the invaders, who become panic-
stricken and flee. The *Chronicle* mentions that the Apostle Santiago gave some help in this affair. This fabulous account has influenced later chronicles and ballads.

Several chronicles followed *The First General Chronicle*. Based
on one of these and on a poem called *Rodrigo* by some and by
others *Las mocedades del Cid* (*The Youthful Deeds of the Cid*)
is *La crónica rimada* (*The Rhymed Chronicle*). This chronicle
purports to give an account of the ancestors of Rodrigo de Vivar,
followed by his exploits during the reign of King Fernando. Indicative of epic degeneration is the narration of a fanciful alliance
formed by the King of France, the Emperor of Germany, and the
Pope. When they demand that Spain pay an annual tribute to the
alliance, King Fernando places Rodrigo in command of an army,
which he leads to the gates of Paris where he defies the twelve
peers of Charlemagne. A truce of four years is finally agreed to by
the contending forces.

In the chronicles which followed *The First General Chronicle*,
especially in *The Rhymed Chronicle*, and in *The Youthful Deeds
of the Cid*, several nonhistorical events appear as attempts are
made by several of the compilers to fill the gaps in the early years
of Rodrigo de Vivar which history and *The Poem of the Cid* leave
blank. These events are reflected later in many ballads, and
through the ballads become the source of a large part of Guillén
de Castro's *Cid I* play. The first of these is Rodrigo's initiation into
armed combat, when, as a stripling of twelve years, he kills Count
Gómez de Gormaz. Jimena, the youngest daughter of the count

appeals to King Fernando with the request that he compel Rodrigo to marry her, a request which the king grants. (The reader will remember that according to history it was King Alfonso who greatly honored Rodrigo by having him marry his niece Jimena.) Rodrigo grudgingly agrees to comply with King Fernando's request that he marry Jimena, but he vows not to live with her until he has become victorious in five battles.

Two of these five battles are the basis for the second of the events just mentioned which, through the ballads, provided Castro with material. Aragon and Castile have a dispute over the city of Calahorra, Aragon claiming that Castile has usurped control of the city. Count Martín González is appointed by the King of Aragon to uphold the latter's right to the city in a trial by combat. Rodrigo de Vivar, the champion of Castile, kills don Martín in the ensuing duel. Rodrigo later defeats five Moorish kings in one battle. A third event used by Castro is Rodrigo's encounter with a leper on a river bank while he is returning to Zamora from a pilgrimage to Santiago. Although his companions shun the pariah, Rodrigo not only helps him to cross the river, but lets him sleep with him under the cover of his waterproof cloak. While Rodrigo is asleep, the leper whispers to him that he is St. Lazarus whom the Lord has sent to breathe upon his shoulder, thereby sending a feeling of warmth through him, with the promise that he will be victorious in any enterprise which he may undertake if at the outset he feels the pervading sensation of warmth.

IV   *The Cid of the Ballads*

A contemporary Spanish scholar, Luis Guarner, has compiled a total of 189 ballads which deal with Rodrigo de Vivar, taken from several well-known collections.[7] Included are ballads which deal with both fictitious and real incidents in the life of the Cid from early childhood until his death in Valencia and burial in Old Castile. *The Rhymed Chronicle* of the Cid goes to extravagant lengths when it has Rodrigo, at the age of twelve, kill Count Gómez de Gormaz. The first ballad in Guarner's collection goes to even more extravagant lengths, for in it Rodrigo, who is not yet ten years of age, functions as a judge and in a serious and lofty tone for one so young, tells of having sent one robber to death on the gallows. But in broad and general terms, the ballads in Guarner's collection parallel the career of Rodrigo de Vivar as narrated in *The*

General Chronicle, including the episode in which his corpse, clad in armor and mounted on his horse Babieca, is led into battle, frightening the troops of King Búcar to such an extent that they flee in panic. The body of the Cid is then conducted to San Pedro de Cardeña for burial there. But at least one other miracle was to be performed by the dead hero, according to one ballad. His life-like, embalmed body, with face and long white beard visible, had been on display for several years in the Monastery of San Pedro de Cardeña. A Jew, musing that no one had ever dared to insult the Cid by pulling his beard, decided that he would do so in order to see what would happen. As he extended his hand to pull the beard, the Cid grasped his sword *Tizona* and withdrew it from its sheath about the breadth of a palm. The terrified Jew immediately fainted. As soon as he regained consciousness he became a Christian, changed his name to Diego Gil, and spent the rest of his life in the monastery in the service of God.

The Spanish ballads were composed by different people in different places at different times. Many underwent gradual changes during the passage of time, as they were transmitted, often orally, from one generation to another. The result is that there is less consistency of treatment in the ballads than there is in the chronicles, which were composed by one author or by a controlled group of writers. This lack of consistency is evident in any collection of ballads in which several of these poems deal with one well-known episode, such as Rodrigo's killing of the count and his marriage to Jimena, daughter of his victim.

One finds in Guarner's collection six ballads which deal with this incident. In two of them, Jimena asks King Fernando to order Rodrigo to marry her as indemnity for the loss of her father. In the other four ballads, she pleads that she be avenged for Rodrigo's outrageous deed. This episode is an important one in Guillén de Castro's *Cid I.* As we have seen, the dramatist develops it as a conflict in Jimena's heart between her love for her fiancé Rodrigo and her filial duty toward her dead father. Incidentally, the historical Jimena Díaz, niece of King Alfonso VI, has become in the chronicles, ballads, and Castro's play the daughter of a fictitious Count Gómez de Gormaz, and she is referred to simply as Jimena Gómez, or as "Jimena Gómez, daughter of Count Lozano." The adjective *lozano,* which meant "vigorous, proud, haughty," apparently was used so often in connection with the fictitious Count of Gormaz that it became converted into a surname.

Great divergence in character and personality can be seen in the various "Cids" who have been dealt with here. The Cid of history and of the epic poem, for example, remained loyal to a monarch who had treated him unjustly and had banished him. His loyalty is all the more remarkable when one considers that, according to medieval law and custom, a vassal who had been banished by his king was justified in taking up arms against him. But Rodrigo de Vivar placed his love for Castile ahead of his own pride. Never obsequious, he refused to resort to flattery, and thus failed to overcome the jealousy which he had aroused in court circles. Underhandedness was no part of his nature, and the account in the epic poem of his deceiving the moneylenders is completely fictitious. Endowed with great drive and energy, scorning personal danger in combat, he was well versed in military strategy and never suffered a crushing defeat. On most occasions he was magnanimous toward his conquered foes. He was a devoted husband and father, a point which is stressed in *The Poem of the Cid*. Extremely superstitious, he believed implicitly in omens as guides. His excellent knowledge of medieval law was unusual in a man whose background was chiefly military.[8]

V *The Cid of the Theater*

It is not surprising that such a famous personage as Rodrigo de Vivar should have inspired many dramatists. At least fourteen plays, including the two by Castro, were written about him in Spain during the Golden Age. Interest in him has continued until the present time, not only in the drama, but in other types of literature as well.[9] But of all the plays which have been written about him in Spanish, none has had as great an influence or received such wide acclaim as Guillén de Castro's *Cid I* and *Cid II*.

CHAPTER 7

Castro's Technique

LOPE de Vega (1562–1635), the creator of the national drama of Spain, gives us in 1609, in his *Arte nuevo de hacer comedias en este tiempo* (*New Art of Writing Plays in This Day and Age*), a general idea of his dramatic theories. He casts aside Classic precepts exemplified by such dramatists as Plautus and Terence, preferring to write the type of play favored by his own generation of theatergoers. He states that a play should reflect contemporary manners. Comedy and tragedy may be mixed. The unity of action should be preserved, but not the unity of time. A play should consist of three acts, the dénouement being delayed until near the end of act three. It is essential that those who play the role of kings and old men, for instance, speak as their counterparts do in real life. Actresses, even when disguised as men, must speak with decorum. The type of verse spoken by the actors should be appropriate to the situation: *décimas* for complaints, sonnets for those who are waiting, *romance* or *octavas* for ordinary discourse, *tercetos* for serious matters, and *redondillas* for love scenes. Deceiving with the truth and equivocal speech are recommended, as are honor situations because of the way in which they move people. Stage costumes should be appropriate to the role played by the actor.

The great Lope, with his incredible command of dramatic technique, his fluid versification, his spontaneity, and his intimate understanding of his fellowman, dominated the drama of his day so completely that most of his contemporary playwrights followed his lead. These dramatists are grouped in what is called "The Dramatic School of Lope de Vega." [1] In a similar fashion, the dramatists of the last few decades of the Golden Age are grouped in what is called "The Dramatic School of Calderón."

I *Certain Major Aspects of Castro's Technique*

Guillén de Castro definitely belongs to Lope's "School." This is not surprising in view of the close friendship which existed between the two and Castro's praise of Lope in several of his plays. Castro makes extensive use of ballads as source material, just as Lope does. Both writers show much in common in their use of verse forms. Castro, like Lope, has an appeal to the common man when he voices objection to royal tyrants, with two cases of regicide in his plays. Both writers condemn the cruelty of Spain's code of honor. But in dramatic craftsmanship, Lope almost always gives evidence of a high level of achievement while Castro often shows considerable unevenness of technique.

At times, in the midst of a pedestrian or banal passage, he will display a flash of inspiration. This feature is apparent in his first play, *Constant Love*. The death scene in Act Three, in which Nísida chooses to die by poison rather than to accept forced marriage to the tyrannical and cruel king, is a welcome contrast to the series of disconnected and uninspired scenes which precede it and is an indication of an as yet undeveloped dramatic talent. In like fashion, a well-written and dramatic passage will be marred by a sudden descent into bathos. *The Count of Irlos* can be taken as an example. Castro follows his ballad source fairly closely until the end of Act Two, when a very inept melodramatic scene of the playwright's own making is introduced. In the ballad, Irlos, long absent from home, has a dream in which he sees his wife in the arms of a prince. Awakening, the count summons his men and announces that it is time for all of them to return to France. Castro elaborates, however, by having the wizard Malgesí cast a spell upon the count, in which he sees Prince Celinos abduct his wife, carry her to the top of a mountain where, sword in hand and grasping her by the hair, he cuts off her head and throws it down to the stage. The count, picking up the seemingly bloody head, rushes toward the mountain as the ground opens and swallows his servant Landín, who, not being under the spell, has seen nothing of what the count has seen. These events must have taxed both the imagination of the audience and the rather crude stage properties of those days.

Critics generally agree that Castro showed considerable skill in his use of ballad material and in the way in which he incorporates entire ballads into his plays. But at times his employment of this material is far from successful, especially when he destroys the continuity of a ballad by distributing its lines among two or more actors. This feature of his technique has already been discussed. The ballads upon which the fictitious histories of the Cid and other epic heroes were based were well known to many of the inhabitants of Spain. Hence, in a play which dealt with an epic hero, the audience would expect the inclusion of certain important ballads, however incongruous and inartistic they might turn out to be in the play itself. This explains in part the inclusion of the incident of the Cid and the leper in the first *Cid* play. In like manner, the inclusion of an episode based upon a well-known ballad detracts considerably from the artistic value of the second *Cid* play. This play is without doubt one of the best which Castro wrote, and insofar as pageantry is concerned, it can rival some of Shakespeare's best historical plays.

The play opens with a battle between the forces of Alfonso and those of Sancho, with the tide of battle shifting from one side to another until Sancho's side is victorious. Later there is the attack on Zamora by Sancho and his followers which ends with the appearance of the ghost of King Fernando who issues a warning to his son. One can also mention the warning which the noble Arias Gonzalo cries out from the walls of besieged Zamora to King Sancho as the latter seems to fall under the sway of the treacherous Bellido Dolfos. Refusal to heed this warning results in the assassination of the king. An especially effective pageant would be the burial procession of the murdered king, as witnessed from the walls of Zamora against the barren background of western Spain. The king's soldiers, all dressed in mourning, march silently by in columns of four, each soldier with unsheathed sword in hand. Then comes the blood-covered corpse of the king on a bier with his crown at his feet and the spear still protruding from his breast. An equally effective pageant would be the famous *reto* issued by Diego Ordóñez de Lara against Zamora and its inhabitants, followed by his duels to the death with three of the sons of Arias Gonzalo who champion the cause of their accused city. The dramatist is at his best in this scene full of pathos as Rodrigo Arias, smitten to the death, his vision clouded, asks his father for assurance that he has been victorious, and still musters sufficient strength to cry out in his dying breath, "Don Diego Ordóñez de

Lara, wait." And finally, one can mention the scene in which King Alfonso, suspected of complicity in the death of his brother, is forced to swear an oath on an iron bolt, a wooden crossbow, and a crucifix that he is innocent of any such charge. After he swears the oath, King Alfonso angrily banishes the Cid. Here indeed are scenes of epic grandeur which would make a superb moving picture which the movie makers have overlooked. In dismal contrast with these scenes, Castro has included the banal romance between Zaida and Alfonso when the latter seeks refuge at the court of the Moorish king of Toledo after his defeat by his brother Sancho.

Especially incongruous is the scene in the garden when the Moors, fearing that the supposedly dormant Alfonso may have overheard an important secret of state, apply the saliva test in order to ascertain whether his sleep is feigned or not. Equally incongruous is the episode in which the hair of the terrified Alfonso rises and then falls as King Alimaimón presses it down, only to rise again when he removes his hand. Perhaps one should not be too severe on Castro, for these are episodes which the audience, familiar with the ballads and chronicles of Spain, would expect to find included in the play. But if Corneille had adapted this play, it seems certain that he would have omitted what were banalities to him (and now to us) just as he omitted the affair of the leper in *Cid I*.

Another characteristic of Castro's technique is his fondness for the melodramatic. Outcasts from society, living in the wilds and dressed as savages, suddenly appear at the crucial moment to save the life of an innocent person, to right a wrong, or to clear up some mystery of long standing. Incidents of this type occur in *Procne and Philomela, The Count of Irlos, The Birth of Montesinos,* and *The Inimical Brothers,* to mention only a few such cases. An especially striking feature of this dramatist's fondness for the melodramatic is his presentation on the stage of scenes of violence in which there is supposedly a visible shedding of blood. One would be justified in referring to this aspect of his technique as a "cult of blood." This fondness for scenes in which blood appears is much in evidence in his first play, *Constant Love*. Nísida cuts her finger on her ring; the king strikes a duke on the head, drawing blood; Celinos, attacked by three assassins, slips in his own blood and later writes a message with the blood which flows from the wound in his chest. In *The Foolish Young Gentleman,* the king slaps a courtier's face, drawing blood; a count, wounded on the head by assailants and weak from loss of blood, is carried onto the stage. Castro seems to have put all restraint aside in his presentation of bloody scenes in *Procne and Philomela.* When Procne comes on the stage for the first time, she has blood on her face. Tereo, angered by Philomela's refusal to accept his advances, draws his dagger in an attempt to cut out her tongue. According to the stage directions, there is "blood shed on the ground." Philomela soon appears with bloody mouth and face. Procne, in order to get revenge for the misdeeds of her husband, kills their son Itis offstage, and then makes her appearance carrying a bloody sword and with blood on her hands. She offers her husband a glass filled with the blood of their child, and when he refuses to drink, she throws the contents into his face. Driante, after killing a lion, appears with his arm covered with blood to the elbow. Teosindo, wounded in battle, enters covered with blood.

Castro's fondness for such scenes continues in *Dido and Aeneas.* The ghost of Siqueo is seen with its face covered with blood. Creusa enters with blood on her face. A bloody sword mysteriously appears. The fall of Troy and the killing of a lion are described in gory detail. Strangely enough, no mention is made of blood when the dying Dido is seen seated on her throne, with her breast pierced by the sword of Aeneas. Scenes of blood play an important part in the first *Cid* play. When Jimena appears before the king in order to demand satisfaction for the death of her father, she carries a handkerchief which has been dipped in his blood. Diego Laínez, in the same scene, appears with his cheek smeared with the blood of the man who had dishonored him. A page enters, carrying a bloody spear. Jimena complains that her garments have been spotted with the blood of her doves which Rodrigo had killed, and Rodrigo, after killing Martín González, returns carrying the latter's head on his spear, which, fortunately, he does not carry onto the stage.

A long chapter could be written about Castro's fondness for bloody scenes. Such scenes are found in twelve of the first fifteen plays in Bruerton's authentic list, and they occur, but with less frequency, in many of the plays of the dramatist's later period. But the last authentic play in Bruerton's list, *The Impoverished Seeker of Royal Favor,* has the following stage direction: "Don

Juan enters, wounded on his left hand and the cuff on his right hand with blood on it."

It is interesting to contrast Castro's technique in presenting scenes of cruelty and violence with that of his avowed master, Lope de Vega, selecting as examples two of the latter's best-known plays, *Fuente Ovejuna* and *Peribáñez y el Comendador de Ocaña*. In *Fuente Ovejuna*, the peasants, driven to desperation by the cruelty and wantonness of their overlord Fernán Gómez, arise *en masse*, and after they have killed him and hacked his body to pieces, they are seen on the stage carrying his head around on a spear. In *Peribáñez y el Comendador de Ocaña*, Peribáñez uses his dagger to kill the knight commander and his two accomplices. But there is no mention of visible blood in either of these plays.[2]

So far in this discussion of Castro's technique, the comments have been rather adverse, attention being called to the author's frequently uneven plot structure, his inability or unwillingness to free himself from the inclusion for modern readers of certain inartistic features of well-known ballads, and his insistence upon presenting bloody scenes on the stage. But there are several aspects of his technique which help to make up for these adverse aspects, one of them being his success in creating several outstanding characters. This does not mean that Castro has created characters who can rival Lope's Peribáñez, Tirso de Molina's don Juan Tenorio, or Ruiz de Alarcón's don Domingo de don Blas. But it does mean that he has created several characters who have an aura of authenticity about them, characters who are entirely human and believable, many of whom give evidence of great moral stature in the face of adverse circumstances. Especially worthy of mention are doña María in *Proud Humility*, the Infanta in *Count Alarcos*, Aurelia in *A Long-Absent Husband Risks Dishonor* (if the play is Castro's), Cecilia and the Princess in *How Much One Esteems One's Honor*, Briseida in *The Inimical Brothers*, and Celaura in *Justice in Mercy*.

But the outstanding individual character in all of Castro's plays is Arias Gonzalo in the second *Cid* play. We see him as the trusted advisor to whom Urraca looks for guidance, a man willing to risk his life in the defense of Zamora when it is besieged by Sancho's troops, unwilling to resort to arms against the person of the king but ready to do so against any followers of the king. Suspecting treachery on the part of Bellido Dolfos and unwilling to connive in Bellido's attempt to free Zamora by assassinating Sancho, from the walls of the besieged city he cries out his famous warning to the king to be on his guard. When it is Zamora's duty to name five champions to defend the honor of their city after it has been accused of complicity in the death of Sancho, Arias Gonzalo volunteers along with his sons. But he insists on being the first one to meet the redoubtable Diego Ordóñez de Lara in the lists. He is well aware that he may be killed by his adversary, but he derives solace from the thought that if the sword of Diego Ordóñez is dulled on him, it will be less deadly when used against his sons. Urraca manages to dissuade him, but only with great difficulty and after many pleas.

Arias Gonzalo is then faced with the terrible duty of naming the order in which his sons will face Diego Ordóñez de Lara. He sees three of them die in the trial by combat, and yet when he swears fealty to King Alfonso, he offers him his two remaining sons if the need should ever arise. Diego Ordóñez had unjustly accused all the inhabitants of Zamora of treason, but when Arias Gonzalo catches sight of him at the ceremony of swearing allegiance to the new king, he remarks in an aside speech which reflects a stoical acceptance of the cruel fate which, because of his position, it was his burden to bear: "This is don Diego de Lara, oh unfortunate Arias Gonzalo, for I can see in his hand the sword which killed my sons! This does not impel me to seek revenge; for his killing them on the field of honor was a misfortune, and misfortunes, while they afflict one, do not entail loss of honor, and so, the sad memory of my sons impels me to tears but not to seek revenge for an affront" (II, 249a).

In her discussion of Lope's technique, Professor Margaret Wilson remarks: "He clearly preferred happy endings, and sometimes even altered his source material in order to achieve them." [3] The same is true of Guillén de Castro, which may seem surprising in view of his penchant for presenting gory scenes on the stage. Thus, the original versions upon which Castro based his *Procne and Philomela, Dangerous Curiosity*, and *Count Alarcos* have tragic endings. But the dramatist, no doubt with his audience in mind, has contrived to give these plays a dénouement of less somber tone. A similar feature can be noted in other plays by this writer.

II *Castro's Comic Figures*

One of the most interesting and most important characters of the Golden Age drama of Spain is the *gracioso* (comic figure). A well-known scholar of the drama of that period does not hesitate to call Lope de Vega's *graciosos* the most sincere and most human characters of his plays.[4] The function of the *gracioso* in the drama is based primarily on a very intimate master-servant relationship. But the *gracioso* is much more than a servant: he counsels, praises, encourages, and at times even chides his master. He is in most cases witty, he is fond of eating and drinking, and is a sly rascal who is not above recourse to devious underhanded measures for pecuniary gain. It is difficult for him to keep a secret, he is often a braggart, but is cowardly at heart. Many times he parodies the actions of his master, and his marriage to the maidservant is one of the marriages with which cloak and sword plays almost always end.[5]

The word *gracioso* appears in the list of characters in only four of the plays that Bruerton considers to be authentic or probably by Castro. These are: *A Long-Absent Husband Risks Dishonor* (1610?–20?); *The Tragedy Caused by Jealousy* (1622); *Mentor to his Own Son* (1620?–23), and *Vice Carried to Extremes* (1623.) Although he is not referred to as *gracioso* in the list of characters, Cotaldo in *The Impoverished Seeker of Royal Favor* is twice given that appellation in the play (II, 414a; 418b). Bruerton places its date between 1620? and 1624. Gonzalo in *The Deceiver Deceived* refers to himself as *gracioso:* "I will go in an angry mood, for to be chicken-hearted is not always a characteristic of the *gracioso*" (III, 177b). Bruerton's dates for this play are 1620?–24. Thus it is seen that the noun *gracioso* is found rather late in Castro's plays as is the case in those of Lope de Vega.

This does not mean, however, that characters who embody the qualifications of the *gracioso* are not to be found in earlier plays by this dramatist. The requisite is that there must be an intimate master-servant relationship throughout the entire work. This requisite is met in every sense by Cobeña in *Truth Ascertained and the Deceptive Marriage* (1608?–12), Gonzalo in *Kinship's Powerful Call* (1613–14), and Tadeo in *The Self-Styled Narcissus* (1612?–15?). Elvira in *The Ill-Mated Couples of Valencia* is an interesting figure who could almost be called a female counterpart of a *gracioso*. Disguised as a page of don Alvaro, who has deceived her into believing that he is not married, she has a role of great importance as she cleverly brings about several amusing complications and finally, disillusioned by the deceptions which she has seen, she decides to enter a convent.

III   *Certain Traits of Castro's Language*

The literary language of the Golden Age saw two fashions—*culteranismo* or *estilo culto* (Cultism) and *conceptismo* (Conceptism)—reach the height of their development. Both movements shun the popular and seek to appeal to a limited group of learned people. The chief exponent of Cultism is Luis de Góngora y Argote (1561–1627) whose name gives us the term *gongorismo* (Gongorism). But one should bear in mind that *culto* is a Latinism from the word *cultus* which means "elegantly expressed" and was current as early as the first century of the Christian era.[6] *Culteranismo*, which is characterized by cultivated obscurity of style and the influence of Latin syntax, is found chiefly in poetry. It is sometimes called "a poetic play on words." *Conceptismo*, with its subtle conceits or strained metaphors and frequent ingenious combinations of ideas, is found chiefly in prose. It is sometimes referred to as "a play on ideas."

Guillén de Castro is not remembered as a great lyric poet, comparable to Lope de Vega or Calderón de la Barca. Beautiful poetic passages can be found in some of his plays, but in general one can say that he was a competent but far from brilliant practitioner of the poetic art. Although the rhetorical figures which are characteristic of *culteranismo* and *conceptismo* appear in his plays, he uses them less frequently and with greater restraint than many of his contemporaries. His treatment of these figures will be taken up in the next few pages.

One feature of *culteranismo* which is found in several writers of the period is the frequent use of metaphors to describe feminine pulchritude. It was a commonplace for them to refer to a woman's eyes as *soles* (suns) or *estrellas* (stars); her tears were *perlas* (pearls) or *aljófar* (dewdrops); her lips were *claveles* (carnations) or *coral* (coral); her cheeks were *rosas* (roses) or *azucenas* (lilies); her white hands were *marfil* (ivory). Metaphors of this type are found in Castro's plays. For example, he refers as follows to women who are weeping: "For when you dim these suns, you give red clouds to your beautiful cheeks and then you take them away" (I, 183a). "Pearls rain down from her eyes more beautiful than the gilded sun" (I, 415a). "Let the downpour cease from the suns which I am courting, the greatest interest of my heart; one has seen it rain while the sun is shining, but one has not seen the sun pour forth rain" (I, 428a).

A woman's eyes can serve as guides: "Have your eyes guide me, since they are stars" (I, 399a). Her mouth and lips provoke typical clichés: "Your mouth has pearls and your lips coral" (II, 276b). "She has ivory in her mouth as well as coral in her lips" (III, 165a).

America, often called *Las Indias*, an expression which came to imply "fabulous wealth," was the source of many metaphors related to feminine beauty: "I saw a woman, and I saw in her a source of great wealth disclosed in the gold of her hair, in the mother-of-pearl of her cheeks, in the pearls of her teeth and the coral of her gums, in the rubies of her lips and another thousand things that are found in this celestial bonanza so that it can compete with Heaven itself" (I, 73b).

A woman appearing before her beloved reminds him of the dawn (II, 58b). Feminine eyes can even outdo our orb of day: "Follow me, and at least in María . . . you will see two suns shine in one day" (II, 565a). The opposite is true when the lady is asleep: "For because she has her two divine morning stars closed, it is like a day without a sun" (II, 85a).

The fact that Castro ridicules timeworn metaphors of this type indicates that he did not take them very seriously: "Provided that you do not call me the sun and my mantilla a storm cloud, you will see that I am not as old as the compliment is" (II, 260b). Ridicule is also provoked by the clichés uttered by two young blades as they see the objects of their affection appear in a window:

MARCELO. I believe that day is dawning now.
OCTAVIO. Suns with such beautiful beams.
HIPOLITA. How tiresome it is to hear the dawn, the sun, the moon and the stars of these compliments, madam.
LEONOR. They are so old that they are stale. (III, 59a)

Culteranismo enriched the language by the introduction of words borrowed from Latin, Greek, and Italian. But when carried to extremes, this resulted in affectation of speech which was ridiculed by many writers, Castro among them. For example, a *gracioso* tells what his special talent is: "I, madam, who improve upon the skill of hyperbolizing whims relevant and sonorous, which means to tell lies, in good Spanish." (*Yo, señora, / que la habilidad abono / de hiperbolicar caprichos / relevantes y sonoros, / que es mentir en buen romance*), III, 276a. It is apparent that translation loses much of the effect of the original Spanish for Castro's audience.

Hyperbaton is one of the most common and most abstruse of the figures of speech which are found in the poetic language of Spain's Golden Age. It is defined as "A figurative construction, transposing or inverting the natural word order." Two examples from English poetry and song are, "When Spring brings back blue days and fair" and "Gone are my friends from the cotton fields away." Of the numerous hiperbata found in the poetry of Góngora, "The Angel of Darkness," one of the most obscure is, *Dos pobres se aparecen pescadores, / nudos al mar de cáñamo fiando,* which, translated word by word is, "Two poor appear fishermen, knots to the sea of hemp trusting," the import of which is, "Two poor fishermen appear, casting their nets into the sea."

The following are typical examples of this figure of speech taken from the plays of Guillén de Castro, who used it in spite of his mockery of *culto* speech: "His clever thought which gave you your understanding more than your arrows sharp" (*Su ingenioso pensamiento, / que te dió el entendimiento / más que tus flechas agudo*), I, 157b. "I will end, because of sadness, beloved son, my life" (*Acabaré, de tristeza, / hijo del alma, la vida*), I, 455b. "I forgive, in order that you will forgive my anger, your deceits" (*Perdono, porque perdones / mi cólera, tus engaños*), II, 478a). "To put of iron around his neck another chain" (*Ponelle de hierro al cuello / otra cadena*), III, 329b.

Another rhetorical figure which is found frequently in the poetry of the period is chiasmus, "An inversion of the order of words or phrases, when repeated or subsequently referred to in a sentence." A less satisfactory definition is "The balancing of the ends against the middle," as in Milton's statement about making "A Heaven of Hell, a Hell of Heaven," or the *Spectator's* pledge "To

enliven morality with wit, to temper wit with morality." The word
"chiasmus" is derived from a Greek word which means "Two lines
placed crosswise." The idea of crossing or inversion is inherent in
every chiasmus, as can be seen by dividing the two examples
given below:

A Heaven of Hell,

a Hell of Heaven.

To enliven morality with wit,

to temper wit with morality.

Castro employed this figure rather frequently: "Don't throw
Heaven to earth, don't raise earth to Heaven." "It is well to do
what he says, but not to say what he does." A double chiasmus is
found in his statement that God's hands can make "the small great
and the great small, the rich poor and the poor rich."

A favorite device of writers of the time was antithesis, which
often turns into oxymoron, a contradictory or incongruous epi-
thet: "Although my breath is of fire, it leaves frozen everything it
touches." "And you will tell her that I kill myself because of what
I saw when I was blind."

One can find in Castro's plays a few examples of anaphora, the
repetition of a word or of words at the beginning of two or more
successive clauses: "Always armed from head to foot; armed I go
to work, armed I return to the village, armed I arrive for dinner,
armed for supper; what is this? And armed I go to bed."

> (*Siempre armado de alto a bajo;*
> *armado voy al trabajo,*
> *armado vuelvo a la aldea,*
> *armado llego a comer,*
> *armado a cenar; ¿qué es esto?*
> *Y armado, ¡par diez! me acuesto.*)   (I, 470b)

Castro at times resorts to ellipsis, the omission of one or more
words, which are obviously understood, but must be supplied to
make the expression grammatically correct. Note the omission of
the verb in the last two sections of "Powerful is your opponent,

and in palace and campaign his opinion the first, and his the best spear."

Dovetailed conversations are found in many Baroque plays, but Castro's use of this device is rather infrequent:

DIDO.   He was a traitor.
ENEAS.   He was in love.
DIDO.   He lost his life.
ENEAS.   He left memories.
DIDO.   He did wrong.
ENEAS.   He enjoyed glories.
DIDO.   He lost them.
ENEAS.   He was unfortunate.
DIDO.   He caused affronts.
ENEAS.   He was in love.

(DIDO.   *Fue traidor.*
ENEAS.   *Fue enamorado.*
DIDO.   *Perdió el ser.*
ENEAS.   *Dejó memorias.*
DIDO.   *Hizo daños.*
ENEAS.   *Gozó glorias.*
DIDO.   *Perdiólas.*
ENEAS.   *Fue desdichado.*
DIDO.   *Causó afrentas.*
ENEAS.   *Tuvo amor.*)   (I, 188b)

Writers of the Baroque period frequently went to excess in the use of the conceit, a metaphor that is meant to be serious, but which is so strained and insipid that the result is bathos. Calderón was one dramatist whose work is marred for modern taste by frequent use of this figure of speech. Castro's use of it is quite limited, the outstanding example being found in his play *The Deceiver Deceived.* A marquis comes upon the Princess of Biarne who, unaware that she is being observed, removes her clothes in preparation for a swim and wades into the water. He describes the scene: "She tosses her clothing into the air. Ah, my Heaven; how well she sets the cold element (water) on fire, and how well does she cast what is warm (her clothes) aside! Is there anyone who will approve such sensible restraint in me, as with strokes of fire she raises snow-white forms (her arms) into the air? How gracefully she cuts the crystal (water) which does not draw

away! Oh, beautiful vessel, without a sail it scorns the sun and
pleads for wind! With what four oars (her limbs) does it skim
through the water, no longer cold!"

> (*Por los aires se despoja*
> *del vestido. ¡Ay, cielo mío;*
> *qué bien abrasa lo frío,*
> *y qué bien lo ardiente arroja!*
> *¡Ay de mí! ¿Quién hay que apruebe*
> *en mí tan cuerdo sosiego,*
> *dando a martirios de fuego*
> *elevaciones de nieve?*
> *¡Qué airosamente divide*
> *el cristal que no recela!*
> *¡Oh, hermoso bajel, sin vela*
> *sol desprecia y viento pide!*
> *¡Con qué cuatro remos boga*
> *por el agua, ya no fría!*) (III, 165b)

Later, in a long gongoristic passage in royal octaves, the marquis gives a detailed description of the scene to some friends, telling how the princess gradually removes her clothes, providing
thereby sharp arrows for the quiver of the blindfolded god
(Cupid), until she enters the water, trusting her pure snow
(white body) to the liquid glass. The sight of this causes the char-
iot of the sun to stop and reverse its course, turning sunset into
dawn, and threatening the ruination of Phoebus. The marquis
calls her *un barco de marfil entre esmeraldas* ("an ivory boat
amidst emeralds") and mentions once more her *nevados remos*
("snow-white oars"). The conceit which compares a person swimming to a vessel, is also found in Calderón. In the latter's metaphor, the arms are oars, the legs the rudder, the nose the prow,
and the eyes two signal lights. Castro, fortunately, limits himself
to one conceit; he calls her limbs *remos* ("oars").

A device which appears at times in literature is "deceiving with
the truth." One of Castro's characters remarks with reference to
this device: "Do you not know that in fact one who deceives with
the truth deceives in a clever fashion?" (*¿Tú no sabes que en efeto
/ engaña como discreto / quien con la verdad engaña?*), II, 484b.
The Princess of Biarne in *The Deceiver Deceived* makes clever
use of this type of deception to disconcert one of her suitors, don

Juan, a marquis, who pretends to be the servant of his younger brother in order to test secretly the worthiness of the princess to become his bride. But despite the efforts of don Juan to keep his identity secret, the princess becomes aware of the fact that he, the supposed servant, is in fact the marquis, her intended husband. She turns the tables on him as she confounds him with the statement: "Love is daring; the marquis will be my husband; you, don Juan, will be my lover" (*Es el amor atrevido; | será el marqués mi marido; | tú, don Juan, serás mi amante*), III, 192a.

It happens occasionally that a writer coins an expression which seems to him so vivid or striking that he becomes enamored of it. Not content with using it once, he is apt to repeat it whenever the occasion presents itself. This is true of Calderón de la Barca whose oxymora *vivo cadáver* ("live corpse"), *esqueleto vivo* ("live skeleton"), and *animado muerto* ("living dead man") appear on more than one occasion in his plays. Guillén de Castro also became enamored of a flowery expression with which a man pays a compliment to a woman in this wise: "What your feet have trod upon I will kiss, as is fitting" (*Lo que han pisado tus plantas | como es justo besaré*), I, 77a. There are several variants of this rather insipid compliment in the works of this dramatist: "And you will leave me under obligation to kiss afterward the ground upon which they have trod" (*Y dejarásme obligado | de que yo bese después | la tierra que hayan pisado*), I, 132b. "Let me place my mouth where you place your feet" (*Déjame poner la boca | donde pones tus pies*), I, 134a. "With my mouth I will sweep what you tread upon" (*Barreré lo que pisas con la boca*), I, 389a.

The expressions quoted above or variants of them appear thirty-five times in the thirty plays which Bruerton considers to be authentic or probably by Castro. Five examples are found in the first act of *The Perfect Knight*. Since expressions like these do not seem to be common to other Golden Age dramatists, the appearance of one or more of them in a play which is of doubtful attribution to Castro would be a strong point in suggesting his authorship.

IV *Other Stylistic Traits*

When writers of the Golden Age expressed such an idea as "to see him," they could choose between the common form *verle* and the less common form *velle* in which the *r* of the infinitive has been assimilated by the *l* of the enclitic pronoun. Also, when expressing such a command as "do it," they could choose between the common form *hacedlo* or the less common metathetic form *haceldo*. Guillén de Castro shows a very strong preference in each case for the less common form. A study based on this preference of the dramatist corroborates most of Bruerton's ascriptions of plays as "Probably by Castro," "Doubtful," and "Texts Not By Castro." [7]

During the Golden Age, plagiarism was common and generally accepted without stigma. Cervantes alludes to this prevalent practice when one of his characters mentions *los intonsos poetas de nuestra edad* ("the unshorn poets of our age"),[8] each of whom is accustomed to write as he wishes and to steal from whomever he likes. Self-plagiarism was also a common practice of many writers of that day. This is not surprising when one considers the relatively short run of most plays and the need to supply the new plays which an avid theatergoing public demanded. Guillén de Castro resorted frequently to self-plagiarism. His fondness for the theme of members of the nobility living as savages in caves and dressed in the skins of wild animals has been touched upon briefly earlier in this study. The noble savages are in general the victims of unjust banishment from society, or they may be the children of nobles, born out of wedlock and reared by peasants, unaware of their noble background. The theme invariably has a happy ending: justice triumphs as the noble savages return to civilized life with all rights restored. Raised in the wilds and developed into mighty hunters, the young men among them have an appeal which Castro's heroines cannot resist, for they show a decided preference for males with outstanding physical prowess. This theme is dealt with in *Constant Love, Procne and Philomela, The Birth of Montesinos, Count Alarcos,* and *The Inimical Brothers.*

Another favorite theme of the playwright is that of the neglected wife who eventually turns the tables on her philandering husband. Castro's source was one of the chronicles based on the history of Aragon. With the aid of a courtier, the neglected wife of King James II deceives her husband into spending the night with her in a dark room, while he has been led to believe that his companion would be the beautiful young wife of a nobleman of Montpeller. Castro develops this theme in *The Perfect Knight, Vice Carried to Extremes,* and *Ingratitude Caused by Love.*

One characteristic of Castro's plays is the frequency with which scenes of violence occur. In six of his plays the violence takes the form of an attack by several assailants against a lone individual, generally a woman. In each instance but one, the following additional features are present: (1) The individual attacked is saved by a stranger or unrecognized person who easily drives the attackers away, giving us the theme of "Rescue by a valiant stranger"; (2) The assailants, with one minor exception, are anonymous insofar as stage directions go; (3) The rescuing stranger turns out to be an unknown relative of the person attacked, or someone closely joined to him by the bonds of past friendship or family interest. This theme is found in *Constant Love, The Happy Revelation, The Birth of Montesinos, The Foolish Young Gentleman, The Count of Irlos,* and *Procne and Philomela.*[9] The first three plays listed above are the first three in Bruerton's list of authentic plays and the latest date assigned by him to any of the remaining three is 1608?–12? Castro apparently had his fill of repeating this theme early in his career.

Castro's feminine characters, in addition to their showing a predilection for men of great physical prowess, often provoke bitter feelings and strife by dropping, with premeditation or not, a token in the midst of a group of young rivals for their affections, each rival being eager to return the token to its owner, even at the cost of a duel. Such situations are found in *The Count of Irlos, The Birth of Montesinos, The Inimical Brothers,* and *The Force of Habit.*

Weddings are generally the occasion for rejoicing and merriment. But three weddings in the plays of Guillén de Castro are the complete opposite of typical weddings. When Marfira, the fiancée of the long-absent Count Irlos, is ordered by Charlemagne to marry Celinos, the unwilling bride-to-be appears for the ceremony dressed in mourning. Count Alarcos, under royal mandate to marry a princess, makes his appearance also dressed in mourning, as does Celaura in *Mercy in Justice.* Examples of self-plagiarism, in addition to the several given in previous paragraphs, are numerous in the works of this playwright, but no others will be included here to illustrate this aspect of his technique.

The literature of Spain is at its best when it is democratic and thus reflects a close relationship between writers or composers and people. Evidence of this is found in the early epic of the Middle Ages, the ballad, and the drama of the Golden Age. In this respect, one should also mention another important democratic feature of Spanish literature—proverbs, since the literature of that nation is undoubtedly as rich in these short pithy sayings as is the literature of any other nation. Cervantes on more than one occasion alludes to them in Don Quijote, remarking that they express the truth since they are maxims drawn from experience. Guillén de Castro, along with most other writers of his day, incorporates numerous proverbs into his works. A few of these, in the form in which the dramatist has adapted them, follow:

If they make a bridge of silver for an enemy who is fleeing.

When one speaks of a despicable person, he comes at once.

For walls covered with hangings have eyes and ears.

Bad news runs fast.

Now indeed they will be able to say that laws go where kings will.

Opportunity gives me its forelock.

For money is a key which closes and opens a mouth.

To think that an outraged woman is changed into a lion!

The proverbial expressions given above have rather close equivalents in English. This is not true, however, of many common Spanish proverbs such as the following: "Hush, and don't say, 'brother, I won't drink any of this water.'" The sense is that many people, when warned of the possible dangers of a course of action, frequently reply: "Such a thing won't happen to me."

A well-known proverb in Spanish is "Pretty women desire the good fortune of a homely woman." This is based on the long-held belief that homely women have happier marriages than beautiful women do. Castro gives us this proverb in reverse when he has a beautiful woman say, "Being unhappy is the only attribute that I have for being beautiful." Along with dozens and dozens of truly proverbial expressions and proverbs which Castro has adapted, one finds in his plays numerous expressions of his own to which he has given a proverbial turn, expressions which do not seem to be found in the standard collections of Spanish proverbs. Some of these are: "No one likes the chain to which he is bound," "To follow the humor of a madman often results in his cure," "The two complain of one pain; it is one and the same molar that aches."

One interesting feature of Spanish writers of the Baroque period is their fondness for puns. Two classes of puns are found in their works: the humorous puns spoken by the *gracioso*, and the *equívoco*, a pun which was meant to be taken seriously and which the author considered to be highly ingenious. Both types of this figure of speech abound in the plays of Guillén de Castro. Rare indeed is the pun which can be translated directly from Spanish into English, but occasionally one can be found. An example of this rare type of pun is found in Castro's *Cid II*, when Zaida and Alonso meet in the garden of King Alimaimón's palace:

ZAIDA.	Alonso, what do you think of the gardens of Toledo?
KING ALONSO.	I can envy them because they are worthy of your plants.
(ZAIDA.	*¿Alonso, qué te parecen*
	los jardines de Toledo?
REY ALONSO.	*Que envidia tenelles puedo*
	de que tus plantas merecen.) (II, 234a)

In order to understand this pun one must bear in mind that *planta* in Spanish means "the sole of the foot" as well as "plant." *Plant* in English, in addition to its botanical usage, has the now obsolete meaning of "sole of the foot."

Castro, like Calderón de la Barca, is inclined to use over and over many of his plays on words. Thus we find *cuerda* meaning "cord, string," or "sensible" used in connection with *atar*, "to tie." *Cuernos* (horns), the sign of cuckoldry, is a favorite with him as is *ola*, "hello" or "wave," with reference to the sea. The homophones *yerro* (error) and *hierro* (iron) are common, as are plays on *grande* (large) or *grandee*, a nobleman. Women are frequently referred to as *ligeras* (light, swift, giddy or even wayward). Some of his puns are of the kind to make a modern reader shudder, as when Leonido, whose name breaks down into León-Ido (Lion-Gone), saves a princess from an attack by a lion, which he drives away and kills. The grateful princess suggests that he is no longer León-Ido but León-Venido (Lion-Come). The *gracioso* Laín is guilty of a feeble pun when he states that a *calvo* (bald man) must be a descendant of the Cid, since one of the Cid's ancestors was Laín Calvo. The following pun in *Constant Love, Donde apenas entre el sol / entrará cuando entre a penas,* is highly reminiscent of a play on words in the first scene of Calderón's *La vida es sueño: y apenas llega, cuando llega a penas.* The respective meaning in each case is that as soon as the sun or a traveler reaches the desired destination, trouble is encountered.

V *Castro's Rural Settings*

Much of the action in Castro's early plays takes place in the wilderness, where the dramatist presents many characters whose main diversion is the chase. In his comments upon the attractions of rustic life, he gives evidence of a greater interest in inanimate nature than one generally finds in writers of the Golden Age. The misogynous Anteo in *The Foolish Young Gentleman* expresses in vigorous terms the pleasures of life in the wilderness:

Clothed in this peasant garb, in this region let me run from the level plain to the summit of the mountain. Here I awake contented, and in the midst of the bright red sky I see the sun rise, I hear the rustling of the wind. I bless the countryside whose grass serves as a carpet; the mountains give me their shelter and the trees their shade. . . . With this life, which seems hard, I live without a care the happier and safer life that God has given me. No lofty thought afflicts my heart, nor do I build towers of vanity upon foundations of ambition. Desire does not torment me, hope does not harm me, a false friend does not deceive me nor does an enemy affront me. I do not bewail dishonor or duels, no rules of conduct offend me, nor do I fear that my wife will dishonor me or show that she is jealous. (I, 51b ff.)

Later, in the same play, Aurora discourses upon the attractions of solitude in a rural setting, mentioning the pleasant sound of a brook, the green of the countryside, the trees which offer shade, flowers and fruit, and the freedom from an affront upon her honor (I, 55b). The wizard Malgesí has praise for a sylvan atmosphere with its pleasant meadow, running water, and song birds (I, 386a). Princess Urraca, after mentioning the many allurements of rustic life, continues with a passage that calls to mind the famous phrase *Beatus ille* of Horace:

Blessed is one who along hidden paths finds diversion in the fields and retires to the mountains. It is not surprising that the queen my mother, with her good taste, finds relief for all her troubles in this country estate. She quit the court, fleeing from its noise and tumult where some take revenge while others cry for justice. (II, 186b)

Atislao, a character in *Mercy in Justice,* also flees to the country in order to escape the noise and bustle of the court (III, 138b), as does Celaura in the same play (III, 148b). Other long passages in Castro's plays in which the charms and attractions of rustic life are brought out are found in *The Deceiver Deceived* (III, 163b; 196b) and in *Mentor to His Own Son* (III, 428b).

VI   *The Social Scene*

Readers are often interested in the picture which a writer gives of his society. While it is true that not all Golden Age dramatists were interested in depicting contemporary manners, it would hardly be possible for a writer to fail to give at least a few hints regarding the society of his day. And when one comes to the Spanish cloak and sword play which deals with the noble and nonnoble classes, the opportunity to glean information about contemporary manners is great indeed. This is especially true in the case of Lope de Vega and Tirso de Molina, whose cloak and sword plays and other types of drama number in the hundreds. Although Guillén de Castro's plays are not nearly as numerous as those of the two dramatists just mentioned, and although not all of them are of the cloak and sword type, he does give his reader a fair amount of information about life in the Spain of his day. Much of this information, however, deals with rather superficial aspects such as dress, cosmetics, and color symbolism.

Spanish dress and fashions in the early part of the seventeenth century were characterized by numerous innovations and a tendency toward excess. Many inhabitants viewed this trend with alarm, activated by fear that the youth of the nation would be demoralized, and these inhabitants exerted pressure on numerous governing bodies to take action. The result was the issuance of numerous sumptuary decrees at both the municipal and national level. One article of dress which aroused considerable opposition was the fluted or ruff collar, which not only required a large amount of cloth, but also had to be starched and placed on a mold before each use. This type of collar, which was both expensive to buy and to launder, was banned by decree early in 1623, in a governmental effort to reduce extravagance of expenditure for personal adornment.

Castro gives us a description of a duke who is getting dressed as servants tie on his collar and straighten it, after which one of them

opens the collar with a mold (II, 412a). Perturbed lest there may
be an excessive amount of bluing (*azul*) on the collar, the duke is
assured by the servant that such is not the case. The fluted collars
seemed difficult to keep in place, for one character remarks that a
person gets tired of straightening them, while another says that
they should be worn so that the head, but not the hair, fits into
them. Indicative of the expense involved in the use of these collars
is the following observation by a *gracioso:* "Office seekers spend
as much on the various ways of having collars opened and in having them put on as they do on shirts" (II, 436a).

Castro does not give a great deal of information about the blue
powder which was used for bluing, and which was one of the
articles banned by governmental decree. He tells us that a
woman's delicate cambric garment is embellished by it, while if a
man has too much of it on his collar, he has the appearance of
going around with his face in a blue plate. The dramatist also has
a comment or two about the uncomfortable cuffs which formed
part of the male attire, but most of his attention and derision is
directed toward the *bigotera*, a device which was worn by men,
generally at night, to train the mustache. A duke, surprised when
he sees his son, a marquis, wearing a *bigotera* while he is getting
dressed, asks:

DUKE.   Is he wounded? What is that thing, son?
MARQUIS. Sir, I am not [wounded].
          (*He removes the* bigotera.)
LAÍN.   If he were, the wound would reach from ear to ear.
MARQUIS. Although it is an annoyance, it is something which is being
          worn now . . .
DUKE.   To think that a grown man would wear such a thing. . . .
          Son, since you follow fashion by wearing it for a while, at
          least do not have it on when you receive visitors.   (III,
          444a)

The *bigotera* was frequently ridiculed by Castro's *graciosos*,
who remark that a man wearing one reminds them of a young
pointer dog that is being trained for hunting. The indications are
that this device first appeared in Spain shortly after 1611, probably in 1612, a premise which can be of use in ascertaining the
date of composition of certain works which have references to
it.[10]

This dramatist tells us very little about women's attire, with brief references to mantillas of two layers of cloth, the long head-dress worn by widows, and the cork-soled clogs (*chapines*), cumbersome articles which were the cause of frequent stumbles and falls. He also mentions the dangerous corrosive sublimate (*solimán*) which ladies applied to their face in order to whiten the skin, ladies who from the neck up are as white as ivory, but the rest of them has the color of walnut.

Comments on etiquette are rather sparse. An impoverished nobleman, seeking a recommendation from a duke who is a stranger to him, becomes incensed because the duke not only did not do him the honor of sitting down to receive him, but also avoided as much as possible addressing him as "Your Grace" (*Vuesa Mercé*), and took pains to see that he and not the impoverished nobleman was the one who terminated the interview. A possible remnant of Moorish influence is seen in the custom of having women be seated on cushions (*almohadas*) rather than on chairs. A chair could be designated, however, as a sign of respect for ladies of the upper ranks of nobility. Thus, when a duchess enters a room accompanied by several noble ladies and maidservants, most of the ladies sit on a divan while the duchess sits on a chair, with her protegée Camila at her feet (II, 523a). In one case, a princess refuses to sit on a chair unless her dear friend Celia also has that privilege. Otherwise, she says, both will sit on cushions. A prince solves the problem by telling the princess: "Well, let them give a chair to Celia, if a cushion does not suffice; it will be a less harmful solution to raise her to your rightful place than to lower you to hers" (II, 110b).

Castro has little to say regarding diversions. Many of his male characters enjoyed hunting, and attendance at theatrical performances is mentioned in several of his plays. He does discuss in detail one parlor game, *letras* (letters of the alphabet), which has much in common with our game of forfeits (II, 456a ff.). He tells us very little about travel and inns, in spite of the fact that Spaniards traveled considerably in those days. His works have occasional references to color symbolism: green for hope, yellow for despair, blue for jealousy. But all in all, when one considers the details which Castro gives of such superficial aspects of his society as dress, cosmetics, and etiquette, his picture of life in Golden Age Spain is far from complete.

Aspects of life which his age considered to have a scientific basis were of greater interest to this dramatist. One such aspect which received wide acceptance in those days is called "natural attraction." It is based on the assumption that people who are related by blood are mysteriously drawn toward one another, even though they are unaware of the fact that they are relatives. In *The Foolish Young Gentleman,* each of two young ladies, Estrella and Aurora, claims that she is the daughter of the king, who has never seen the face of his daughter until then. So the king is confronted with the dilemma of deciding which of the two is telling the truth. He decides to resolve the matter by embracing each of the claimants. His reaction is negative when he embraces Estrella, but when he embraces Aurora, he remarks: "The wings of my heart tell me that you are in it. It wants to come forth to receive part of its noble blood; come closer to me, lest it should come forth, for it is struggling to do so" (I, 77a).

By means of natural attraction, Honorio, in *Kinship's Powerful Call,* learns that the child Luisico, whom his horse has trampled, is his grandson, and natural attraction proves which of two young men had seduced Lidora, and consequently, is the father of Luisico. This theory also plays an important part in clearing up matters of consanguinity in several other plays by Castro, among them *Constant Love, Count Alarcos,* and *The Impoverished Seeker of Royal Favor.* But the limits of credibility are breached when Enrique, a young man who has never seen Grimaltos and is unaware that the latter is his father, undergoes a noticeable inner reaction merely upon hearing his name mentioned (I, 448a).

Some people in Castro's time realized that marriage between cousins could be fraught with danger, but apparently not everyone was willing to accept that theory:

TEODORA. Are you not aware that marriage between cousins can portend danger?

CELIA. Such mad thoughts, although accepted, are fallacious; rather by measuring the pattern of pleasure with fate, the blood which is the same in two people, if it is mingled, reacts with greater force. (II, 93a)

In Castro's plays, marriages between two people who are related by blood generally turn out well. But such is not true of marriages between people whose blood does not have an affinity. This explains why Procne's marriage to Tereo is bound to be unhappy: "Oh marriage arranged for at an evil hour! For it is an infernal torment to mix haphazardly two bloods of different warmth in which nature is in conflict with pleasure and vanquishes beauty" (I, 128b).

Since a child's noble blood could be damaged by a wet nurse, Jaime Centellas states that his wife nursed their son Miguel rather than risk possible harm to the baby: "His own mother nursed him, perturbed by the fact that at times the poor milk of a wet nurse ruins good blood, for in my opinion, sir, this is the hidden cause which explains the lack of noble blood in those who have a noble heritage" (II, 138a).

VII   *Science and Other Details in Castro's Thought*

Astrology was considered to be a respectable science during the sixteenth and seventeenth centuries, thus continuing a belief long held that a person's status in life depended upon the position of the stars when he was born. This belief had the support of the Bible, and to reject it was to question Holy Writ. But astrology with its emphasis on fatalism ran counter to free will. The result was a compromise accepted by many Golden Age writers that the stars inclined the will but did not have the power to force it. This compromise is reflected in a few of Castro's plays:

AMBASSADOR.   Surprisingly up to now I did not believe that which you have told; the king has given too much credit to astrology.

DUKE.   Those who foresee danger are sensible and prudent, because the Supreme Judge has our lives written in the stars.

AMBASSADOR.   And does anyone know how to read them?

DUKE.   Sometimes. And, in short, these things are of such nature if they are closely scrutinized, that to believe them is folly and to fear them is prudence.   (I, 48b)

A firm belief is expressed in *Cid II* that the influence of the stars can be overcome:

ALIMAIMÓN. Toledo is to be captured?
2ND MOOR. So is it written in Heaven; but your care and prudence
will triumph over astrology, because wisdom is stronger
than its influence.   (II, 235a)

Closely tied to the acceptance of astrology as a science was a widespread belief in omens, although the authorities of the Church were strong in their condemnation of such a belief. Omens, which generally portend disaster, play a part in several of Castro's plays, especially *Constant Love, Procne and Philomela* and *The Tragedy Caused by Jealousy*. Mirrors break without being touched, precious stones suddenly leave their setting without any sign of an external force, dogs howl, and owls croak. Procne has a dream in which she takes out her heart and gives it to her husband, who eats it bit by bit. This dream presages the murder by her of her son, and her feeding the heart of the child to its father. The king, in *The Tragedy Caused by Jealousy*, while on a hunt, sees an eagle which carries a white dove in its beak. When he shoots the eagle, he is spattered with blood as the dove falls dead at his feet. This ominous event, coupled with the singing by a peasant of an old ballad based on the tragic death of Inés de Castro, arouses a feeling of apprehension within him. Hastening to his clandestine assignation with Margarita, he finds that she has been murdered by his jealous queen.[11]

One important aspect of the intellectual life of the Golden Age which held a great attraction for Guillén de Castro was the theme of "El Perfecto Caballero" ("The Perfect Knight"). This theme has intrigued Spanish writers from the very beginning of the nation's literature. It is dealt with in *Partida II* of *Las Siete Partidas,* a code of law composed under the supervision of Alfonso el Sabio, which was finished *ca.* 1265. Juan Manuel, the nephew of Alfonso el Sabio, takes up this topic in three of his works in prose. The theme is discussed by the unknown author of the *Libro de Alexandre,* a work of the thirteenth century, and it plays an important part in the Romances of Chivalry. During the Renaissance, numerous works in Italy, France and England, as well as in Spain, were written about the qualities of the Perfect Knight. The best known of these is Castiglione's *Il Cortegiano (The Courtier),* published in 1528 and translated into Spanish by Juan Boscán in

1534. *Il Cortegiano* has had considerable influence upon Spanish writers of the Renaissance and Golden Age.[12]

In a primitive Spanish epic poem, the *Cantar de los Infantes de Lara* (*Song of the Princes of Lara*), we find mentioned seven traits which summarize the qualities of the Perfect Knight: loyalty, justice, truth, valor, fidelity, generosity, and a fondness for good company.[13] Boscán's friend, the courtier and poet Garcilaso de la Vega, who was trained in equitation, the manipulation of weapons and music as well as in Latin, Greek, French and Italian, is the outstanding example of the Perfect Knight in Spain during the Renaissance. Guillén de Castro, in his play *The Perfect Knight*, has a long account of the training given by don Jaime Centellas to his son Miguel, in order to help the youngster develop into the Perfect Knight which he typifies in the play. A summary of this training follows:

After the child was weaned, his food and drink were carefully controlled. He was taught Christian Doctrine without delay, and at the age of five he began to attend school, with attendance at Mass preceding each visit to school. He learned to read and to write moderately well, which suffices for a noble gentleman. When the son continued his education beyond the elementary level, the father insisted that corporal punishment should never be inflicted upon him, because corporal punishment may have the effect of causing a child to suffer affronts without avenging them. Oral castigation is better fitted for a well-inclined youngster, and no punishment is effective on a youngster who is not well inclined. The father states that he laid hands on his son only once, and then because the boy had told a lie. Later Miguel received instruction in equitation, the manipulation of weapons, and in dueling.

On his twentieth birthday, after receiving communion, he became a knight and received several admonitions from his father. He should remember to keep God continually in his thoughts, he should avoid evil companions, and should be courteous. He should have many friends but very few intimate ones. He should pay his just debts, and should not resort to subterfuge if he is not able to pay them. Gambling should be avoided, but if he does gamble, he should pay his gambling debts and keep his promises. Women should be avoided, but if he does have relations with them, it should be with moderation. If he serves the king as a soldier, it is his duty to obey his superiors. If a duel is forced upon him, he must not flee when attacked, but should kill or be killed. He should avenge affronts and learn to keep a secret at all costs. Since he is poor he should not marry, but if he does, he should look for wealth in his wife's qualities and for beauty in her reputation. If he follows these admonitions, God will make of him a Perfect Knight (II, 138a ff.).

In the play itself, Miguel, whose mother was a Cardona, and who was related to the noble Viques and Moncadas, displays many of the attributes of the Perfect Knight. He is a skillful hunter, an excellent swordsman, and brave in battle. His handsome figure, noble conduct and courtesy attract attention, especially among the ladies. Generous toward his father, he is guided by the Spanish code of honor which leads him to refuse to violate palace decorum or to act disloyally against the king in the involved love intrigue which centers around Diana, Ludovico, and the King and Queen of Naples. So impressive are Miguel's actions, bearing, loyalty, and fondness for the truth that the general reaction of the characters with whom he comes in contact in the play is to refer to him as a "Perfect Knight."

When Grimaltos, in *The Birth of Montesinos,* has been banished from the kingdom, he and his wife retire to the wilderness with their son Montesinos. Grimaltos constantly impresses upon his son the obligations of a knight. He must fulfill his promises, avoid evil things, be moderate in his relations with women, be humble, self-controlled, and polite. He should not gamble, but if he does, let him do it quietly and without any unfair advantage. An affront to his honor must be avenged, he should keep secrets and defend the faith of Christ by word and deed (I, 438a). Montesinos also receives from his father detailed instructions about dueling (I, 439b).

Carlos, the son of Count Alarcos, has also been reared in the wilderness, and he too is trained in a manner that befits a Perfect Knight. First of all comes acceptance of God and a belief in Christianity. He must shun unseemly actions, he should be neither lavish nor miserly with money, and in his relations with women he should be pleasant, but have love for none. His promises must be kept, he must keep secrets which are entrusted to him. He should avoid situations which can involve him in a duel, but if he is involved in one, he should not flinch. He should also be a loyal friend and always tell the truth (II, 26a).

Guillén de Castro presents Rodrigo de Bivar, the Cid, as an example of the concept of the Perfect Knight in Golden Age Spain. Of noble descent, young Rodrigo does not hesitate to risk his life in a duel with Count Lozano in order to avenge the affront committed against the honor of his father and of his family. In doing so, he chooses honor over his love for Jimena. Brave in battle, loyal to his unjust monarch, he leads his troops against the infidel Moors. In his personal habits he is moderate in eating and drinking, and avoids the use of profanity. He is above all a practicing Christian, saying grace before meals, setting a Christian attitude for his men, and showing real Christian charity toward the leper.[14] Less flamboyant but more credible as a Perfect Knight is Arias Gonzalo who plays such an important role in the second *Cid* play.

Castro, in common with most Spanish writers of the sixteenth and seventeenth centuries who dealt with the theme of the Perfect Knight, placed great emphasis upon his being first and foremost a person who not only expressed an acceptance of the Roman Catholic doctrines of his day, but also put them into practice. This is brought out by quotations from two of his plays: "With this and with the Law of Christ kept strong as a rock in his heart and speech, and which he must defend both by word and sword, he will possess honor" (I, 438b).

MARGARITA. And tell me, what attributes must a good knight have in order to appear to be one?
CARLOS.   To be first of all a good Christian.   (II, 26a)

When don Pedro in *The Force of Habit* hands his sword to his son, he impresses upon him the duty of a knight to defend his faith with his sword and to be ready to die for it (III, 46b).

While the Spanish Perfect Knight is religious, the Italian Renaissance gentleman is not. Pauline Marshall notes that from the qualifications which Castiglione assigns to the Perfect Courtier, religion is omitted entirely, although the Prince must love God. "But having, as it were, thrown a sop to the Church and to religion in general, the far-from-pious group at the court of Urbino passes on to other matters. . . . Thus it will be seen that for the *caballero perfecto* religion is a vital force, as it had been to the man of the Middle Ages. It will also be seen that to don Alonso the 'Christian religion' is Roman Catholicism. There is a marked difference between the Italian Renaissance Courtier, whose deepest veneration is for beauty, and the seventeenth-century Spanish Courtier, whose religious devotion is portrayed so deeply rooted that it constantly affects his behaviour." [15] The counterpart of the *caballero perfecto* in France was the *honnête homme* ("honest man, honorable man, gentleman, courtier"). But in him, as in the Italian Perfect Courtier, religion plays a minor role.

CHAPTER 8

Castro's Influence

I Among his Contemporaries

ALTHOUGH Guillén de Castro is ranked with the minor dramatists of the Golden Age, and in spite of the rather limited number of plays which he wrote, he did exert a fair amount of influence upon the literary life of his day. Mention has been made earlier of the praise accorded him by Lope de Vega. Cervantes mentions him in his *Viaje al Parnaso*. He also received favorable mention from Rojas Villandrando and Pérez de Montalbán. His election to membership in the *Academia Poética* of Madrid would seem to indicate the approval of at least some of the outstanding writers of the time. His play *The Self-Styled Narcissus* inspired Moreto's *El lindo don Diego* (*The Foppish Don Diego*). Although critics in general express the opinion that Moreto's play is superior to Castro's, it is undeniable that Castro's play has excellent qualities. Juliá Martínez, in his edition of the plays of this dramatist, calls attention to the influence of his *Procne and Philomela* upon Rojas Zorrilla's play of the same name (I, lxi) and also (III, xvi) to the influence of Castro's *Mercy in Justice* upon Rojas Zorrilla's *No hay ser padre siendo Rey* (*One Cannot Act as a Father if he is King.*)

Juliá Martínez on more than one occasion calls attention to what he considers to be the influence of Guillén de Castro upon Calderón de la Barca: ". . . In any case it will make us think of the times when one can perceive signs that Calderón must have read the works of Guillén de Castro with considerable pleasure" (II, xxi). Juliá Martínez sees a possible relationship between a passage in Castro's *How Much One Esteems One's Honor* and a passage in Calderón's *Life is a Dream* (III, vi-vii). In his comments upon *The Self-Styled Narcissus*, the editor reiterates: "The sonnet *Apenas tiene pluma el avecilla* in which one can see a slight analogy with the monologue of Segismundo in the first act of *La vida es sueño* furnishes us with another suspicion that Calderón read the works of Castro with pleasure" (III, xv). Angel Valbuena Prat also calls attention to a possible influence of Castro upon Calderón.[1]

One of Castro's earliest plays, *The Foolish Young Gentleman,* which Bruerton dates 1595?–1605?, has so many points in common with Calderón's *Life is a Dream,* that it is highly probable that Calderón did borrow several details from it when he composed his masterpiece. The scene of *The Foolish Young Gentleman* is Hungary. The two leading female characters are Aurora, a princess, and Estrella, whose father is a nobleman. Perturbed by several sinister portents which preceded the birth of Aurora, the king asks his wise men for advice. Their judgment is that no man should look upon Aurora's face until she is married. Otherwise, never-ending calamities will assail the world. The king orders a fortress to be built in the mountains, where the princess is kept, accompanied only by Estrella and two maids. Unauthorized entrance to the region is forbidden and several guards are stationed there. Whenever Aurora leaves the fortress, her face is masked. Several years pass. Warfare develops between the forces of Hungary and an army led by Estrella's father. Estrella is a "general" in the forces which oppose her father, while Aurora is a "general" in the forces which oppose *her* father.

The scene of *Life is a Dream* is Poland. The two leading female characters are Estrella, a princess, and Rosaura, daughter of a nobleman. (A. E. Sloman, in his edition of this play, notes that Rosaura is an anagram of Auroras.) Several sinister portents precede the birth of Prince Segismundo, whose horoscope indicates that he will be bold, cruel, and the cause of great dissension in the land. In order to forestall such harm to the realm, the king has a small tower built in an isolated region in the mountains, entrance to which is forbidden. There Segismundo lives in chains, with only Clotaldo as his companion, plus a few guards whom he sees only when they are masked. Segismundo eventually leads an army against his father. Estrella joins the forces of the king, while Rosaura fights on the side of Segismundo.

Several minor parallels between the two plays can also be noted. When Anteo and Segismundo appear on the stage for the first time, each is dressed in the skins of animals. Anteo says that the sound of a trumpet or drum makes his hair stand on end;

Segismundo, in the palace, says that military music is the only kind which he wants to hear. In both plays there is considerable punning on Estrella's name. Lotario, in Castro's play, upon seeing the face of the beautiful Estrella for the first time, remarks, "but how can I kill you, when not seeing you will kill me?" (*mas, ¿cómo podré matarte | cuando me mata el no verte?*"), I, 54b. In a similar vein, Segismundo, when he sees Rosaura for the first time, tells her: "But let me see you and die; for I do not know, now that I am smitten, if looking at you slays me, what would not being able to look at you do to me?" (*Pero véate yo y muera; | que no sé, rendido, ya, | si el verte muerte me da, | el no verte ¿qué me diera?*"), vv. 233–36.

II *Castro in the Eighteenth Century*

Guillén de Castro enjoyed considerable popularity during the first half of the seventeenth century, but his works, along with the Golden Age drama in general, lost favor in Spain with the adherents of French Neoclassic theories during the eighteenth century. Between 1786 and 1819, Guillén de Castro's *The Youthful Deeds of the Cid* was presented at least four times in Madrid. But during the same period there were at least two performances in Madrid of Corneille's *Le Cid* and at least twelve performances of Spanish translations of Corneille's work.[2] Emilio Cotarelo y Mori lists seven performances in Madrid of *The Youthful Deeds of the Cid* between 1793 and 1819, as well as numerous performances of plays with such titles as *Don Rodrigo de Vivar, La afrenta del Cid,* and *La tragedia del Cid.*[3] No other play which Bruerton considers to be authentic Castro is mentioned.

III *Castro and the Romanticists*

Toward the end of the eighteenth century and early in the nineteenth century, German and English Romanticists became aware of the beauties of the Spanish ballads and the high qualities of the Golden Age drama. Several British writers, among them Thomas Rodd, John H. Frere, Sir Walter Scott, Byron, Lord Holland, and John G. Lockhart not only read the ballads in Spanish, but translated many of them into English.[4] Several ballads which dealt with Rodrigo de Vivar, the Cid, attracted the attention of Lord Holland, who had spent some time in Spain and who was familiar with some of the drama of Spain's Golden Age. He was also interested in Lope de Vega and Guillén de Castro, about whom he wrote a two-volume work.[5] In his discussion of Castro's first *Cid* play, he lists eight ballads which deal with the great Spanish hero and translates them into English verse. When he compares the qualities of the first *Cid* play and Corneille's *Le Cid*, he states that Corneille gives evidence of superior judgment by omitting several grotesque and disgusting incidents which are found in Castro's play. The omission of these incidents constitutes the chief merit of the celebrated French tragedy, which is also superior in the credibility of plot and the general elevation of style. But he asserts that neither Lope de Vega nor Calderón has in any one work combined natural sentiments and poetical language with truly tragical situations so successfully as Guillén de Castro did in *Cid I*. Lord Holland can see nothing good in the second *Cid* play, saying that it is mediocre for the most part and lacking in unity and verisimilitude. He is especially appalled by the circumstances of King Sancho's assassination.

IV   *Castro in Recent Years*

Interest in Castro's plays during the past hundred years or so has been limited for the most part to the two *Cid* plays, especially *Cid I*. Listed in a bibliography compiled under the direction of José Simón Díaz are thirty-three editions of either one or both *Cid* plays in various languages, and nineteen studies which have been based upon these editions.[6] In the recent past, several studies deal with or are based in part on *Cid I*. One of the most important of these studies is *Wölfflin's Principles in Spanish Drama: 1500–1700* (New York, 1952), by Darnell H. Roaten and F. Sánchez y Escribano. In his *Principles of Art History* (see Bibliography for title in German), Wölfflin has arranged in five contrasting pairs the categories which he developed to characterize and contrast the plastic arts of the Renaissance and the Baroque. Roaten and Sánchez y Escribano transfer and apply Wölfflin's categories to literature, especially the drama of the sixteenth and seventeenth centuries in Spain, after first calling attention to the close relationship which existed between painting and literature during those days.

Three plays of the Renaissance are analyzed in the light of these five categories. The authors then analyze in a similar manner three plays of the Baroque period: Lope de Vega's *Fuente Ove-*

juna, Guillén de Castro's *Las mocedades del Cid, comedia primera,* and Calderón de la Barca's *La vida es sueño.* Their discussion of Castro's play (pp. 134–60) begins with the listing of the main theme—Rodrigo, the Christian Knight, and three subplots: Rodrigo-Jimena; Rodrigo-Urraca; King-don Sancho. Then they take up one by one the five contrasting categories which differentiate Baroque Drama from Renaissance Drama.

Although not all critics may agree that the main theme of *Cid I* is "Rodrigo, the Christian Knight," Roaten and Sánchez y Escribano stress this point again and again in their discussion of the play. Their point of view is well expressed in the following quotation: "The leper scene contains the kernel of the ideological teaching of the play. The central point around which the serious theater revolved was religion: everything had some relation to the divine. The object of *Las mocedades del Cid* is to exalt Rodrigo as the faultless Christian knight. To the aggressively religious seventeenth century and especially to the people of Spain, the crowning glory of the knight was devotion to Christianity. The presence of the leper functions to bestow this piety on the Cid" (p. 143). And again: "For a full understanding of the play as an outgrowth of seventeenth-century Spanish culture, it is essential to realize also that Rodrigo is a fusion of the secular and the religious, an epitome of both the knight and the Christian" (pp. 158–59).

Pedro Salinas, in an article which deals with the sword in *Cid I,* "La espada y los tiempos de la vida en *Las mocedades del Cid,*" pp. 151–57 of *Ensayos de la literatura hispánica del Cantar del Mió Cid a García Lorca* (Madrid, 1958), calls attention to the fact that the sword frequently served to signify or to symbolize. He notes that the word *espada* (sword) appears more than forty times in the play, but he limits his discussion to three situations which signify adolescence, youth, and old age—the bestowing of the sword upon Rodrigo when he becomes a knight, Sancho's eagerness to reach the age when he too can wield a sword, and the bitter realization of Diego Laínez that he is too old and decrepit to wield his sword in order to regain his lost honor. The cycle ends: the sword transmits to us three distinct, real, and psychological ages of man, the drama of life from dawn to sunset.

Symbolic objects in *Cid I* are also discussed by Charles A. McBride in "Los objetos materiales como objetos significativos en *Las mocedades del Cid,*" *Nueva Revista de Filología Hispánica,* XV

(1961), 448–58. Among the objects mentioned is the sword of Mudarra, which Rodrigo plans to use when he faces the man who dishonored his father. Here the sword symbolizes individual and national honor as well as vengeance. But when Diego Laínez, after he has been dishonored by Count Lozano, hangs his sword unsheathed upon the wall, we see in his act a symbol of the shame which has come upon him.

The role of divine justice in *Cid I* and *Cid II* is the theme of an article by Sturgis E. Leavitt, "Divine Justice in the *Hazañas del Cid*," *Hispania*, XII (1929), 141–46. The author mentions several warnings which the impetuous Prince Sancho receives, among them the prediction of his horoscope that he will be killed by a hurled weapon and that someone closely related to him will be the cause; Prince Sancho's confrontation with the ghost of his father at the siege of Zamora and the warning of Arias Gonzalo that he should not trust the traitorous Bellido Dolfos. Heaven chooses Bellido to be its agent, and when Sancho asks him to hold his spear, the instrument of vengeance and the agent of retribution have been brought together.

John G. Weiger deals with the theme of silence in *Cid I* in "Los silencios de *Las mocedades del Cid*," *Hispanófila*, 23 (1965), 1–7. Act I is "the act of the great silences," Act II, "the act of the great noises," and Act III, "the act of the lack of silence."

John G. Weiger, in a thought-provoking article, "Sobre la originalidad e independencia de Guillén de Castro," *Hispanófila*, 31 (September, 1967), 1–15, argues that in many cases in which Castro is said to show originality and independence, regicide in *Constant Love*, for example, he is in reality adapting his situations to Lope de Vega's concept of "The New Comedy." This article is based on material from *Constant Love, The Ill-Mated Couples of Valencia, Dangerous Curiosity*, the two *Cid* plays, and *The Honorable Poor Nobleman*.

William C. McCrary calls attention to a new trend in criticism of Castro's *Cid I*—emphasis upon the art of the play rather than upon Corneille's adaptation or the *romance* tradition. His analysis of the play, "Guillén de Castro and the *Moçedades* of Rodrigo: A Study of Tradition and Innovation" in *Romance Studies in Memory of Edward Billings Ham* (Hayward, California, 1967), pp. 89–102, ". . . is an attempt to examine what the dramatist took from the earlier legends, what he added and modified, and how he organized his materials according to a specific design, in an effort to appraise the art—the *poesis*—of the play" (p. 89). Especially important in the gradual transformation of Rodrigo from a private individual into a redeemer figure is the episode of the leper, which ". . . is, in effect, a 'nativity scene' which heralds the birth of the national hero of Spain" (p. 97). Roaten and Sánchez y Escribano have also called attention to the importance of this episode, which Corneille, no doubt with his audience in mind, omitted from his adaptation. In McCrary's opinion, "The image of Rodrigo as Castro defines it in the *Moçedades* represents an accommodation of the medieval legends to the universal hero myth of which David, in particular, is an example" (pp. 98–99). The author closes with the statement that ". . . Castro has realized an extraordinary graceful accommodation of the *mocedades* legends to the catholic blueprint of the hero" (p. 102).

An exceedingly important and illuminating interpretation of *Cid I* is Russell P. Sebold's "Un David español, o 'Galán Divino': El Cid Contrarreformista de Guillén de Castro," pp. 217–42 of *Homage to John M. Hill. In Memoriam* (Madrid, 1968). The author cites numerous parallels between Rodrigo de Vivar and the David of biblical history; for instance, Diego Laínez, the father of Rodrigo, and Jesse, the father of David, have points in common; Rodrigo's brothers prove to be cowards when tested by their father, and David's cowardly brothers refuse to meet Goliath in a trial by combat; the youthful Rodrigo and David in their first duel kill a formidable opponent; a dispute between the Castilians and the Aragonese, and one between the Israelites and Philistines is settled by a trial by combat between two individuals, after which each victor decapitates his victim; both Rodrigo and David refuse to gird on a sword which is offered to them, and in each case the victor who has defeated the giant is rewarded by marriage to a young lady of high rank.

During the sixteenth and seventeenth centuries in Spain, David personified the heroic struggle of the just to gain salvation by force of arms. David was also identified with Christ, of whom he was called a "Precursor." He was also known for his help to the poor and needy. Rodrigo, with his Christian militancy and other traits, is metamorphosed by Castro into a "Spanish David."

The arrogant, proud Cid as he appears in certain ballads, refusing to kiss the hand of his king and threatening the Pope, could not be accepted as the incarnation of Spanish values during the Counter-Reformation. So Castro suppressed these adverse traits and gave new virtues to his hero. For example, salvation is gained by good works as well as faith, which explains Castro's treatment of the episode of the leper.

Rodrigo, like David, begins as a warrior in the physical sense, and becomes a warrior in the spiritual sense, thereby symbolizing the universal struggle for salvation.

The studies which have just been summarized are additional proof that interest in Castro's dramatic production is in general limited to *Cid I* and *Cid II*.[7] The disparity between the interest in these two plays and the remaining plays is indeed striking. If one excepts the three-volume edition by Juliá Martínez, most of the remaining works have been edited only once, often in a perfunctory manner. The limitation of interest in Castro's plays to *Cid I* and *Cid II* is in a certain sense understandable, since he is known chiefly for the first of these two works. But a few of his lesser-known plays are worthy indeed of scholarly editions. Among these one can mention *The Perfect Knight* and *The Deceiver Deceived*.[8] The Juliá Martínez edition, which lacks explanatory notes, is not satisfactory for students who fail to have a background in the drama of the Golden Age. What should be available are annotated editions of a few of his plays similar to Víctor Said Armesto's edition of *Cid I* and *Cid II* in Spanish, or G. W. Umphrey's edition of *Cid I* in English.

V *Epilogue*

Until the past few years, students of the Spanish drama, dazzled by the greatness of Lope de Vega and Calderón de la Barca, have failed to appreciate the contributions which Guillén de Castro has made to the development of the *comedia*. But it is becoming increasingly evident that his contributions have been rather substantial. One can mention in this respect his adaptations of ballad material in which he is second only to Lope de Vega. His contribution to an understanding of the code of honor is considerable, especially when he is rightfully classed with other writers who call attention to many of the code's inhuman and cruel aspects. Scattered throughout his plays are numerous important comments which throw light upon the Spanish concept of the Perfect Knight. His *Don Quijote de la Mancha* and *Dangerous Curi-*

osity seem to be the earliest dramatizations of Cervantes' great novel. Recent investigations call attention to the skillful construction which is manifest in his first *Cid* play.

Insofar as special studies are concerned, there is much work to be done on Castro's plays before we have a fairly complete picture of his role in the development of the Golden Age drama. Still to be investigated thoroughly is the extent to which Castro, the most important dramatist of the Valencian School, influenced Lope and his "New Comedy." Angel Valbuena Prat refers specifically to *cierto sabor prelopista* ("a certain pre-Lopean savor") when he discusses Castro's two *Cid* plays.[9] Also still awaiting penetrating scholarly attention is the extent of Castro's influence upon Calderón and other contemporary dramatists. According to Professor Margaret Wilson, Castro's dramatizations of marital conflict ". . . open the way for such later masterpieces as Lope's *El castigo sin venganza* and the great honour tragedies of Calderón."[10]

A play based upon the conflict between love and honor can have universal appeal. But it must be admitted that Castro's *Cid I*, in spite of its skillful construction, does not have such appeal, for it reflects a code of conduct which readers in general can neither appreciate nor accept. Certain episodes in the play (the Cid and the leper, for instance), while they may reflect the spirit of the age in Spain, also detract from its appeal to the general reader. To most students of world drama, Castro will continue to be known as the author of the play upon which the first great French Classic tragedy is based. So even if he failed to produce a masterpiece, he inspired one, which is considerable glory in itself.

Notes and References

Chapter One

1. Rinaldo Froldi, *Il teatro valenzano e l'origine della commedia barocca* (Pisa, 1962).

2. Otis H. Green, *Spain and the Western Tradition*, I (Madison, 1963), 279.

3. See D. Pedro Salvá, *Cancionero de la Academia de los Nocturnos estractado de sus actas originales,* ed. Francisco Martí Grajales (Valencia, 1905–1906), 4 vols. For Castro's list of contributions to the *Academia,* see IV, 196–97. Considerable biographical information about the dramatist is given in an appendix to III, 119–79.

4. José Sánchez, *Academias literarias del siglo de oro español* (Madrid, 1961), p. 222.

5. Matrimony in Castro's plays is discussed at some length in the following articles by John G. Weiger: "Another Look at the Biography of Guillén de Castro," *Bulletin of the Comediantes,* X (Spring, 1958), 3–5; "Matrimony in the Theatre of Guillén de Castro," *op. cit.,* X (Fall, 1958), 1–3; "Forced Marriage in Castro's Theatre," *op. cit.,* XV (Fall, 1963), 1–4. See also Robert R. La Du, "A Rejoinder to: Matrimony in the Theatre of Guillén de Castro," *op. cit.,* XI (Fall, 1959), 10–16.

6. Otis H. Green, "New Documents for the Biography of Guillén de Castro y Bellvis," *Revue Hispanique,* LXXXI, Part II (1933), 260.

7. *Obras de Don Guillén de Castro y Bellvis,* ed. Eduardo Juliá Martínez (Madrid, 1925–1927), I, xvii–xxii. Hereinafter referred to as *Obras.* Volume and page references to Castro's plays and comments by Juliá Martínez will be to this edition unless otherwise stated.

8. "The Chronology of the *Comedias* of Guillén de Castro," *Hispanic Review,* XII (1944), 90. The plays in the two *Partes,* plus *La tragedia por los celos* (*The Tragedy Caused by Jealousy*), add up to only twenty-five plays. Bruerton apparently forgot to mention *Constant Love* and *The Foolish Young Gentleman,* which, added to the twenty-five plays, give his figure of twenty-seven authentic plays. He includes the two plays last mentioned in his list of "Authentic Plays."

9. Bruerton, pp. 150–51. The translations of these titles and transla-

tions in the remaining part of this study are by the present writer unless otherwise stated.

Chapter Two

1. Agustín Durán, *Romancero General,* Biblioteca de Autores Españoles, X (Madrid, 1851), 254b. The second part of Durán's collection is found in Vol. XVI of this set.

2. Durán, X, 257b.

3. *Ibid.,* 224b.

4. Fernando del Pulgar, *Claros varones de Castilla,* Clásicos Castellanos, 49 (Madrid, 1923), 72.

5. The name Talabote may well refer to the redoubtable English hero, Talbot, one of the characters in Shakespeare's *The First Part of King Henry VI.* Pulgar seems to have confused Talabote with the English champion Count Huntingdon. See Pulgar, p. 73, note 1.

6. *El ingenioso hidalgo Don Quijote de la Mancha,* Clásicos Castellanos, 8 (Madrid, 1934), 215. Juliá Martínez, II, 517b.

7. Manuel de Montolíu, in *El alma de España y sus reflejos en la literatura del siglo de oro* (Barcelona, 1942), pp. 328–29, discusses the failure of many of the contemporaries of Cervantes to recognize the great hidden qualities of his masterpiece, since they interpret the work as parodical rather than satirical, burlesque rather than ironical. Alberto Navarro González expresses a much more favorable opinion of Castro's adaptation of this great novel than the present writer does. He states that in spite of the ridiculous scene in which don Quijote tries to swim across the stage, Castro has been successful in expressing not only manifest exterior qualities, but also profound and detailed traits such as the generous and lofty motives of the noble gentleman. See his "Dos estudios. I. El ingenioso Don Quixote en la España del siglo XVII. II. El ingenioso Don Quijote, caballero andante, cristiano y santo," *Anales Cervantinos,* VI (1957), 18–19 and *passim.*

8. Durán, X, 198a.

9. *Ibid.,* 324b.

10. *Ibid.,* 325a.

11. Marcelino Menéndez y Pelayo, *Antología de poetas líricos castellanos* (Madrid, 1899), VIII, 202. A variant of this ballad is found in Durán, XVI, 207b.

Chapter Three

1. Juan Díaz Rengifo, *Arte Poética* (Barcelona, 1759), p. 33.

2. Bruerton, pp. 98–113.

3. S. Griswold Morley and Courtney Bruerton, *The Chronology of Lope de Vega's "Comedias"* (New York and London, 1940), p. 13.

4. *Hispanic Review,* VII (1939), 235.

5. William E. Wilson, *"Bigoteras* and the Date of Lope's *El cuerdo en su casa," Bulletin of the Comediantes,* VII, No. 2, (Fall, 1955), 31.

6. An investigation of the orthoëpy of the so-called "Authentic Castro Plays" and those of doubtful attribution to him may shed considerable light on the question of authorship. J. H. Arjona, in a study of this type, "Two Plays Attributed to Lope de Vega and Guillén de Castro," *Hispanic Review,* XXXIII (1965), 387–94, expresses the belief that Castro wrote *A Long-Absent Husband Risks Dishonor,* and that Lope was the author of *The Siege of Tremecen.* Arjona justifiably criticizes the findings of the present writer in his article "The Orthoëpy of Certain Words in the Plays of Guillén de Castro," *Hispanic Review,* XXI (1953), 146–50. This study is based on a mechanical rather than a rhythmic scanning of Castro's verses and is of but slight value in determining the question of authorship.

Chapter Four

1. George T. Northup, *Three Plays by Calderón* (Boston, 1926), pp. xvi–xxiv. Two of the laws of the honor code which are listed by Northup, "Secrecy is the best solution" and "For a secret offense, a secret revenge," are indicative of the great efforts which would be taken to keep the loss of one's honor from becoming public knowledge, since one's reputation was thereby lost. This is brought out by John G. Weiger in his dissertation, *The Relationship of Honor, "Fama" and Death in the Valencian Drama of the Golden Age* (Indiana University, 1966). Weiger finds ". . . that there is a close relationship not only between the concepts of *honor* and *honra,* but between *honra* and one's reputation or *fama.* So closely linked are *honra* and *fama* that at times they are indistinguishable. . . . To be without *honra* is considered an untenable position. Consequently, *honra* becomes the basis for existence and worth the risk of one's life. It follows, then, that *fama* is likewise something for which one is willing to lay down one's life" (p. 4). Weiger calls attention to one dual aspect of honor in the Golden Age: *Honor* is an intrinsic quality in man; *honra* is *honor* when it becomes publicly known (p. 3). Américo Castro remarks that the use of the word *honra* in the title of Calderón's play *El médico de su honra* (*The Surgeon of His Honor*) refers to *honor* which is no longer intact. He also calls attention to the fact that one spoke more often of *deshonra* than of *deshonor* (*De la edad conflictiva. I. El drama de la honra en España y en su literatura* [Madrid, 1961]), pp. 55–56. This seems logical, since the pejorative prefix *des-* with its meaning of "deprivation" is more fittingly used with *honra* referring to *honor* that has been blemished. Weiger, however, finds that in the Valencian

dramatists the words *honor* and *honra* seem to be used interchangeably, and that the concepts denoted by them are interrelated (pp. 309-11).

2. William E. Wilson, "Guillén de Castro and the Codification of Honor," *Bulletin of the Comediantes*, XIX (Spring, 1967), 24b ff.

3. "Un dramaturgo de la Edad de Oro: Guillén de Castro. Notas a un sector de su teatro," *Revista de Filología Española*, XXVIII (1944), 390-91.

4. "Honra y duelo," *Romanistisches Jahrbuch*, III (1950), 404.

5. George T. Northup, p. xx.

6. Alfonso García Valdecasas, *El hidalgo y el honor* (Madrid, 1948), p. 182.

7. *Don Quijote de la Mancha*, Clásicos Castellanos, 8 (Madrid, 1934), 192 and note 12.

8. An excellent analysis of this play is given by Everett W. Hesse in his *Calderón de la Barca* (New York: Twayne Publishers, Inc., 1967), pp. 110-22.

9. Comments on Cervantes' opposition to certain features of the code of honor can be found in G. T. Northup, "Cervantes' Attitude Toward Honor," *Modern Philology*, XXI (1923-1924), 397-421; Américo Castro, *El pensamiento de Cervantes* (Madrid, 1925), pp. 361-83. García Valdecasas, in *El hidalgo y el honor*, pp. 215-24, gives a brief discussion of adverse comments on the honor code by Cervantes, Lope de Vega, Ruiz de Alarcón, Moreto, Gracián, and Calderón. See also W. J. Entwistle, "Honra y duelo," pp. 404-20, for several comments in Calderón's plays on the injustice and cruelty of the code. A recent dissertation by Peter Podol, *Criticism of the Honor Code in the Spanish Theatre* (University of Pennsylvania, 1968), has a few brief references to two plays by Castro and to two plays sometimes attributed to him.

10. *La fuerza de la sangre* in *Obras completas*, vol. 13, *Novelas Ejemplares* II, ed. Schevill and Bonilla (Madrid, 1923), 126-27.

11. See Northup's edition of *Three Plays by Calderón*, pp. xvii, xxi. The editor, unfortunately, does not state where references to these aspects can be found in Calderón's plays.

12. Américo Castro, *De la edad conflictiva. I. El drama de la honra en España y en su literatura* (Madrid, 1961), pp. 21, 27.

13. *Three Plays by Calderón*, p. xxii.

14. "Honra y duelo," p. 407.

15. "El doble aspecto de la honra en el teatro del siglo XVII," *Hispanic Review*, XXVI (1958), 99-101. See also Gustavo Correa, "El doble aspecto de la honra en *Peribáñez y el Comendador de Ocaña*," *Hispanic Review*, XXVI (1958), 188-99. The dual aspect of honor is

also discussed by Wilfredo Casanova in "Honor, patrimonio del alma y opinión social, patrimonio de casta en *El Alcalde de Zalamea,* de Calderón," *Hispanófila,* 33 (Mayo, 1968), 17–33. He states that there is an "exterior honor," based on class conventions and the fear of losing one's reputation, and an "interior honor," of spiritual order which is found in every male of the Golden Age who could claim that he was without taint of Moorish or Jewish blood. For the "Patrimony of the Soul" he owed allegiance only to God.

16. *Three Plays by Calderón,* p. xxii.

17. "Honor in Golden-Age Drama: Its Relation to Real Life and Morals," *Bulletin of Hispanic Studies,* XXXV (October, 1958), 200.

18. The discussion of honor in this chapter has been limited more or less to its treatment in Castro's plays. The matter is quite complex and has received considerable attention from scholars in recent years. Those readers who wish to gain a more detailed insight into the problem, especially those who have little or no reading knowledge of Spanish, will find the following articles to be interesting and instructive: C. A. Jones, "Honor in *El alcalde de Zalamea,*" *Modern Language Review,* L (1955), 444–49; P. N. Dunn, "Honour and the Christian Background in Calderón, *Bulletin of Hispanic Studies,* XXXVII (1960), 75–105: P. N. Dunn, "Patrimonio del alma," *Bulletin of Hispanic Studies,* XLI (1964), 78–85.

Chapter Five

1. Durán, X, 503a.

2. *Ibid.,* 479a.

3. *Ibid.,* 480a.

4. *Ibid.,* 485a.

5. *Ibid.*

6. The granting of the title "Cid" to Rodrigo by the king is mentioned in ballads 753 and 754 of Durán's collection (p. 493). The title apparently was fairly common, and was applied to Christians who had lived among the Moors or to those who had Moorish vassals. See R. Menéndez Pidal, *Cantar de Mió Cid,* II: Vocabulario (Madrid, 1945), 574.

7. Durán, X, 484b ff.

8. G. W. Umphrey, ed., *Las mocedades del Cid por Guillén de Castro* (New York, 1939), p. 155.

9. Durán, X, 484a. The first eight lines of this ballad, no. 734, have been omitted.

10. *Ibid.,* 488a.

11. Ballad no. 744, Durán, X, 489, deals with the duel between Rodrigo and Martín González. Castro bases little, if any, of his account

on this ballad, which has the duel take place at some indefinite time after Rodrigo has married Jimena. The Cid defeats and beheads his enemy.

12. See, for example, A. A. Parker, *The Approach to the Spanish Drama of the Golden Age,* no. VI in the Diamante Series, (London, 1957); Arnold G. Reichenberger, "The Uniqueness of the *Comedia,*" *Hispanic Review,* XXVII (1959), 303–16; Gerald E. Wade, "The Interpretation of the *Comedia,*" *Bulletin of the Comediantes,* XI (Spring, 1959), 1–6; Stephen Gilman, "The *Comedia* in the light of Recent Criticism Including the New Criticism," *Bulletin of the Comediantes,* XII (Spring, 1960), 1–5; Karl-Ludwig Selig, "Some Remarks on the *Comedia* and New Criticism," *Bulletin of the Comediantes,* XII (Spring, 1960), 12–13; Eric Bentley, "The Universality of the Comedia," *Hispanic Review,* XXXVIII (April, 1970), 147–62. The rejoinder of Professor Reichenberger to the article just mentioned is found in the same issue of *Hispanic Review,* pp. 163–73.

13. Joaquín Casalduero, *Estudios sobre el teatro español* (Madrid, 1962), pp. 47–48.

14. C. H. C. Wright, *A History of French Literature* (New York, 1925), p. 306.

15. *Le Cid,* ed. L. Lejealle and J. Dubois, Librairie Larousse (Paris, 1965), p. 10.

16. Henry Carrington Lancaster, *A History of French Dramatic Literature in the Seventeenth Century. Part II, The Period of Corneille, 1635–1651* (Baltimore-London-Paris, 1932), I, 123.

17. *D. Guillén de Castro, Las mocedades del Cid,* Said Armesto, ed., Segunda Edición, *Clásicos Castellanos,* 15 (Madrid, 1923), viii.

18. *La Comedia espagnole en France de Hardy à Racine* (Paris, 1900), pp. 205–6. See page 214 of this work for the comments of Adolf F. von Schack, a German critic, who finds *Le Cid* of Corneille to be greatly inferior to Castro's play.

19. *Études sur l'Espagne, Première Série* (Paris, 1895), pp. 43–44.

20. In addition to Said Armesto's comments, see, for example, Julio Cejador y Frauca, *Historia de la lengua y literatura castellana* (Madrid, 1916), IV, 187–88; Manuel de Montolíu, *Literatura castellana* (Barcelona, 1929), pp. 646–47 and F. C. Sainz de Robles, *El teatro español. Historia y antología* (Madrid, 1943), IV, 24. A notable exception is Angel Valbuena Prat, who remarks that an evaluation parallel between the two works will be vain, since we have two masterpieces, one which reflects the dynamism of the school of Lope de Vega, and the other, French neoclassicism of the seventeenth century: *Historia de la literatura española* (Barcelona, 1960), II, 379–80. The following works are suggested for a more detailed study of the two plays: Adalbert Hämel, *Der Cid im Spanischen Drama des XVI und XVII Jahrhunderts* (Halle

a. S., 1910); Jole Scudieri Ruggieri, "*Le Cid* di Corneille e *Las mocedades del Cid* di Guillén de Castro," *Archivum Romanicum*, XIV (1930), 1–79; Walther Küchler, "Streifzüge durch die Spanische Comedia. II: Über die Cid-Dramen von Guillen de Castro und Corneille," *Die neuren Sprachen*, XXXIX (1931), 503–12; Wilfried Floeck, *Las mocedades del Cid von Guillén de Castro und Le Cid von Pierre Corneille, Ein neuer Vergleich* (Bonn; Romanisches Seminar der Universität, 1969.)

21. George Ticknor, *History of Spanish Literature*, Fourth American Edition (Boston, 1872), II, 358–59.

22. James Fitzmaurice-Kelly, *Chapters on Spanish Literature* (London, 1908), p. 24.

23. George T. Northup, *An Introduction to Spanish Literature* (Chicago, 1925), p. 283.

24. Durán, X, 498a.

25. *Ibid.*, 504b.

26. *Ibid.*, 524b.

27. *Ibid.*, 503b.

28. The *reto* of Diego Ordóñez de Lara is dealt with in ballads 787, 789, 790, 791 in Durán, X, 509–11. Castro's account, which is longer than that found in any of these ballads, seems to appropriate details from more than one of them and to include a few original details of his own.

29. Durán, X, 509b.

30. *The Chronicle of the Cid* (New York, 1958), p. 29.

31. Durán, X, 500ab.

32. *Ibid.*, 513ab.

33. *Ibid.*, 514b.

34. *Ibid.*, 515a.

35. *Ibid.*

36. *Ibid.*, 515b.

37. *Ibid.*, 524ab. Professor S. G. Morley, who includes a ballad almost identical with this one in his *Spanish Ballads* (New York, 1938), states (p. 153) that it ". . . is probably related to a degenerate form of the *Cantar del Cerco de Zamora* . . . ; but the exaggerated details of the king's threatened punishment seem to be an invention of this *romancerista*, as also the strange symbols of the *cerrojo* [bolt of iron] and *ballesta* [crossbow]. In the *Iª crónica* Alfonso swears upon a Bible."

38. Durán, X, 199a.

Chapter Six

1. Ramón Menéndez Pidal, *La España del Cid* (Madrid, 1929), I, 203 ff. See 204, note 2, for a list of sources of this incident.

2. *Ibid.*, 221.

3. *European Literature and the Latin Middle Ages,* trans. Willard R. Trask (New York, 1953), p. 386.

4. See Menéndez Pidal's edition of the *Poema de Mió Cid,* Clásicos Castellanos, 24 (Madrid, 1913), "Elementos ficticios," 31–38, and his *La España del Cid,* II, 593–600.

5. For a recent book on The Learned King, see John Keller, *Alfonso X, el Sabio* (New York: Twayne Publishers, Inc., 1967). *La primera crónica general* has been edited in *Nueva Biblioteca de Autores Españoles,* V (Madrid, 1906).

6. Menéndez Pidal, *La España del Cid,* I, 197; 211.

7. *Romancero del Cid precedido del 'Cantar de Rodrigo'* (Valladolid, 1954.)

8. Ramón Menéndez Pidal, the outstanding authority on the Cid, gives a rather detailed account of the character of the historical Rodrigo de Vivar in *La España del Cid,* II, 633–44. In the same work, I, 32–62, he calls attention to the unscholarly prejudiced views of such detractors of the Cid as Masdeu and Dozy.

9. See Adalbert Hämel, *Der Cid im Spanischen Drama des XVI und XVII Jahrhunderts* (Halle a. S., 1910), pp. 1–14, 107–9, and Jole Scudieri Ruggieri, *La leggenda del Cid nella letteratura spagnola* (Modena, 1947), pp. 9–26.

Chapter Seven

1. Numerous comments on Lope's dramatic technique will be found in Francis C. Hayes, *Lope de Vega* (New York: Twayne Publishers, Inc., 1967), pp. 63–104, and in Margaret Wilson, *Spanish Drama of the Golden Age* (Oxford: Pergamon Press, 1969), pp. 56–83.

2. Sturgis E. Leavitt, in his article "Some Aspects of the Grotesque in the Drama of the *Siglo de Oro,*" *Hispania,* XVIII (1935), 77–86, calls attention to the appearance of such things as lions, dragons, bulls, and snakes on the stage of that day. He also mentions scenes of blood and horror in a few of Lope's plays and in three plays by Guillén de Castro. He states that "Calderón, in whom the drama of the century reaches its climax, is literally steeped in gore" (p. 85). But it would seem that the title of "Most Gory Dramatist of the Golden Age" belongs to Guillén de Castro rather than to Calderón.

3. Margaret Wilson, p. 69.

4. J. H. Arjona, "La introducción del gracioso en el teatro de Lope de Vega," *Hispanic Review,* VII, 1. The *gracioso* evolved in Lope de Vega's plays some time before the noun *gracioso* was applied to him in the list of characters. Thus, in the earliest plays by Lope, the *gracioso* is frequently called *criado* (servant) or *lacayo* (lackey) in the list of characters, or else no statement is made concerning his role. This

explains the difficulty which faces scholars in their attempts to designate Lope's first real *gracioso*.

5. J. H. Arjona lists in his article thirty traits of Tristán, whom he considers to be Lope's first *gracioso*, although he is not so called in the list of characters in *La francesilla*, the play in which he appears. Morley and Bruerton give 1595–1598 as the date of composition of this play.

6. Ernst Robert Curtius, *European Literature and the Latin Middle Ages* (New York, N. Y., 1963), p. 294, n. 56.

7. W. E. Wilson, "A Note on Fifteen Plays Attributed to Guillén de Castro," *Modern Language Quarterly*, VIII (1947), 393–400.

8. *Don Quijote de la Mancha*, Clásicos Castellanos, 22, Segunda edición (Madrid, 1935), 274 and note to line 24.

9. W. E. Wilson, "Two Recurring Themes in Castro's Plays," *Bulletin of the Comediantes*, IX (Fall, 1957), 25–27.

10. W. E. Wilson, "Two Notes on Guillén de Castro," *Hispanic Review*, XVIII (1950), 63–66, and "*Bigoteras* and the Date of *El cuerdo en su casa*," *Bulletin of the Comediantes*, VII (Fall, 1955), 29–31.

11. Castro's use of omens is dealt with in L. L. Barrett's "The Omen in Guillén de Castro's Drama," *Hispania*, XXII (1939), 73–78. For an illuminating discussion of astrology and omens in Spain during the Renaissance and the Baroque Period, see Otis H. Green, *Spain and the Western Tradition*, II, 227–52. The ballad in which the king hears the peasant sing in *The Tragedy Caused by Jealousy* is an interesting example of kledonomancy. Otis H. Green discusses this type of omen on pages 237 ff.

12. For a list of early Spanish treatises on courtesy and The Perfect Knight, see Pauline Marshall, *El caballero perfecto de Alonso Jerónimo de Salas Barbadillo* (Boulder, 1949), pp. x–xxii.

13. Otis H. Green, *Spain and the Western Tradition*, I, 10.

14. The Cid as an exemplar of The Perfect Knight is discussed by Darnell H. Roaten and F. Sánchez y Escribano in *Wölfflin's Principles in Spanish Drama, 1500–1700* (New York, 1952), pp. 134–47.

15. *Op. cit.*, p. xliii.

Chapter Eight

1. *Historia del teatro español* (Barcelona, 1956), p. 130.

2. Ada M. Coe, "Catálogo bibliográfico y crítico de las comedias anunciadas en los periódicos de Madrid desde 1661 hasta 1819," *The Johns Hopkins Studies in Romance Literatures and Language. Extra Volume IX* (Baltimore-Oxford, 1935), 44.

3. *Isidoro Maiquez y el teatro de su tiempo* (Madrid, 1902), pp. 574–837.

4. See Erasmo Buceta, "Traducciones inglesas de romances en el primer tercio del siglo XIX," *Revue Hispanique*, LXII (1924), 459–555.

5. Henry Richard Lord Holland, *Some Account of the Lives and Writings of Lope de Vega Carpio and Guillen de Castro* (London, 1817), 2 vols. Volume II deals almost exclusively with Castro.

6. *Bibliografía de la literatura hispánica*, vol. 7 (Madrid, 1967), 713–34.

7. Castro's two *Cid* plays are still being performed in Spain. *Cid I* was paired with Corneille's *Le Cid* in a bilingual program of corresponding scenes from each play in Madrid in 1967. (See *Bulletin of the Comediantes*, XX [Spring, 1968], 23a.) A production of *Las mocedades del Cid* which combined *Parts I* and *II* had several performances in Madrid between November, 1968 and February, 1969. (*Bulletin of the Comediantes*, XXI [Spring, 1969], 32b.)

8. For an edition of one of Castro's plays and a play which it inspired, see *Guillén de Castro "El Narciso en su opinión"* / *Agustín Moreto "El lindo don Diego,"* ed. Alva V. Ebersole (Madrid, 1968).

9. *Historia del teatro español*, p. 128.

10. *Spanish Drama of the Golden Age*, p. 141.

Selected Bibliography

A. Useful Editions of Castro's Plays

Obras de don Guillén de Castro y Bellvis. Edited by Eduardo Juliá Martínez. 3 vols. (Madrid: Imprenta de la "Revista de Archivos, Bibliotecas y Museos," 1925–1927). This is the only complete modern edition of Castro's plays and poetry. Several of the forty-five plays included are of doubtful ascription to the dramatist. Has long introduction and comments upon each play. Students who do not have considerable background in Golden Age drama will be hampered by the lack of explanatory notes.

D. Guillén de Castro. Las mocedades del Cid. Edited by Víctor Said Armesto (Madrid: Ediciones de "La Lectura," 1923), *Clásicos Castellanos,* 15, 2nd ed. Excellent edition of the two *Cid* plays with introduction and copious notes. Given in footnotes is the location in Durán's collection of each ballad upon which these plays are based.

Las mocedades del Cid por Guillén de Castro. Edited by George W. Umphrey (New York: Henry Holt and Company, 1939). Helpful introduction and notes in English with vocabulary. Nine ballads from Durán's collection are included either entire or in part in a special section.

Las mocedades del Cid in *Diez Comedias del Siglo de Oro.* Edited by Hymen Alpern and José Martel (New York: Harper and Brothers Publishers, 1939). Revision by Leonard Mades (1968). Revised text has short commentary on Castro, metrical scheme of *Cid I,* and some footnotes on the play.

Las mocedades del Cid in *Spanish Drama of the Golden Age.* Edited by Raymond R. MacCurdy (New York: Appleton-Century-Crofts, 1971). This edition of *Cid I* has a short chronology and discussion of Castro and his plays along with a selected bibliography and metrical scheme. Numerous footnotes accompany the text.

La leggenda del Cid nella letteratura spagnola. Las mocedades del Cid di Guillén de Castro y Bellvis. Edited by Jole Scudieri Ruggieri (Modena: Società Tipografica Modense, 1947). Has a brief but valuable introduction which deals with Castro's *Cid I* and its influence in Spain and abroad. The text of *Cid I* is given, but without notes.

The Youthful Deeds of the Cid. Prose translation of *Cid I* and *Cid II* by Robert R. La Du, Luis Soto-Ruiz and Giles A. Daeger, with introduction by John G. Weiger (New York: Exposition Press, 1969).

B. Periodical Articles

ARJONA, J. H. "La introducción del *gracioso* en el teatro de Lope de Vega," *Hispanic Review,* VII (1939), 1–21. Lists several characteristics of Tristán, who is perhaps Lope's first *gracioso.*

————. "Two Plays Attributed to Lope de Vega and Guillén de Castro," *Hispanic Review,* XXXIII (1965), 387–94. Verse evidence indicates that Castro wrote *A Long-Absent Husband Risks Dishonor* and that Lope wrote *The Siege of Tremecen.*

BARRETT, L. L. "The Omen in Guillén de Castro's Drama," *Hispania,* XXII (1939), 73–78. Calls attention to Castro's skill in his use of supernatural phenomena in his plays.

BENTLEY, ERIC. "The Universality of the *Comedia,*" *Hispanic Review,* XXXVIII (1970), 147–62. Stresses the view that the *Comedia* is not unique, but universal in its appeal.

BRUERTON, COURTNEY. "The Chronology of the *Comedias* of Guillén de Castro," *Hispanic Review,* XII (1944), 89–151. This outstanding study of Castro's versification casts doubt upon the authenticity of twelve plays attributed to him.

BUCETA, ERASMO. "Traducciones inglesas de romances en el primer tercio del siglo XIX," *Revue Hispanique,* LXII (1924), 459–555. Deals with the interest of Robert Southey, Sir Walter Scott, Lord Byron, J. G. Lockhart, and other Hispanophiles in the ballads of Spain. Several translations of ballads are included.

CASANOVA, WILFREDO O. "Honor, patrimonio del alma y opinión social, patrimonio de casta en *El alcalde de Zalamea,* de Calderón," *Hispanófila,* 33 (1968), 17–33. There is an "exterior honor" based on class conventions and an "interior honor" or "patrimony of the soul" for which one owes allegiance only to God.

COE, ADA M. "Catálogo bibliográfico y crítico de las comedias anunciadas en los periódicos de Madrid desde 1661 hasta 1819," *The Johns Hopkins Studies in Romance Literatures and Languages, Extra Volume IX* (1935), 1–270. Lists a few performances of Castro's *Cid* plays and performances of French translations of *Cid I.*

CORREA, GUSTAVO. "El doble aspecto de la honra en el teatro del siglo XVII," *Hispanic Review,* XXVI (1958), 99–107. "Vertical Honor" is inherent in one's social position; "Horizontal Honor" reflects the complex interrelations among the members of the community.

———. "El doble aspecto de la honra en *Peribáñez y el Comendador de Ocaña*," *Hispanic Review*, XXVI (1958), 188–99. The author applies his theory of "Vertical Honor" and "Horizontal Honor" to this play by Lope de Vega.

DUNN, PETER N. "Honour and the Christian Background in Calderón," *Bulletin of Hispanic Studies*, XXXVII (1960), 75–105. Discusses traditional view that Calderón's honor plays are immoral and whether these plays may be considered in Christian terms.

———. "Patrimonio del alma," *Bulletin of Hispanic Studies*, XLI (1964), 78–85. A discussion of natural and divine law in Calderón's *El alcalde de Zalamea*.

ENTWISTLE, WILLIAM J. "Honra y duelo," *Romanistisches Jahrbuch*, III (1950), 404–20. Comments on the laws of the duel, because these are the laws that govern all the attitudes of a gentleman in contact with his peers.

GILMAN, STEPHEN. "The *Comedia* in the Light of Recent Criticism including the New Criticism," *Bulletin of the Comediantes*, XII (Spring, 1960), 1–5. Poetry should not be divorced from historical human experience.

GREEN, OTIS H. "New Documents for the Biography of Guillén de Castro y Bellvis," *Revue Hispanique*, LXXXI, Part II (1933), 248–60. A reconstruction of Castro's activities between 1609 and 1616.

JONES, C. A. "Honor in *El alcalde de Zalamea*," *The Modern Language Review*, L (1955), 444–49. The peasant Pedro Crespo exemplifies honor as "Patrimony of the Soul," and the soul is God's alone.

———. "Honour in Golden Age Drama: its Relation to Real Life and Morals," *Bulletin of Hispanic Studies*, XXXV (1958), 199–210. The author is of the opinion that there is more than a little fiction in the treatment of honor in Golden Age plays.

KENNEDY, RUTH LEE. "Moretiana," *Hispanic Review*, VII (1939), 225–236. Establishes the date of composition of Castro's *The Greatest Spouse* as some time after 1617.

LA DU, ROBERT R. "A Rejoinder to: Matrimony in the Theatre of Guillén de Castro," *Bulletin of the Comediantes*, XI (Fall, 1959), 10–16. Forced marriages in Castro's plays do not always end unhappily.

LEAVITT, STURGIS E. "Some Aspects of the Grotesque in the Drama of the *Siglo de Oro*," *Hispania*, XVIII (1935), 77–86. Discussed are some horrible events in *Procne and Philomela, Dido and Aeneas, The Count of Irlos, Proud Humility,* and *Count Alarcos.*

MCBRIDE, CHARLES A. "Los objetos materiales como objetos significativos en *Las mocedades del Cid,*" *Nueva Revista de Filología Hispánica,* XV (1961), 448–58. The sword as a symbol of honor, vengeance, and shame.

MCCRARY, WILLIAM C. "Guillén de Castro and the *Moçedades of Rodrigo: A Study of Tradition and Innovation,*" in *Romance Studies in Memory of Edward Billings Ham* (Hayward-California: California State College Publications, no. 2, 1967), 89–102. Emphasis upon the art of the play rather than upon the adaptation by Corneille.

NAVARRO GONZÁLEZ, ALBERTO. "Dos Estudios. I. El ingenioso don Quijote en la España del siglo XVII," *Anales Cervantinos,* VI (1957), 1–48. Praises Castro for being the first to bring the real spirit of don Quijote to the stage.

NORTHUP, GEORGE T. "Cervantes' Attitude Toward Honor," *Modern Philology,* 21 (1923–1924), 397–421. Discusses protests of Cervantes against the cruel aspects of the code of honor, while he accepts everything in it that is noble and generous.

REICHENBERGER, ARNOLD G. "The Uniqueness of the *Comedia,*" *Hispanic Review,* XXVII (1959), 303–16. Expresses the opinion that the *Comedia* is great because it is an unsurpassed instrument of self-expression of a people.

————. "The Uniqueness of the *Comedia,*" *Hispanic Review,* XXXVIII (1970), 163–73. Reiterates that the *Comedia* is unique in expressing the convictions and ideals held by all elements of Spanish society from the king down.

ROCA FRANQUESA, JOSÉ MARÍA. "Un dramaturgo de la edad de oro: Guillén de Castro. Notas a un sector de su teatro," *Revista de Filología Española,* XXVIII (1944), 378–427. Calls Castro's theme of regicide "a daring thesis."

SALINAS, PEDRO. "La espada y los tiempos de la vida en *Las mocedades del Cid,*" pp. 151–57 of *Ensayos de la literatura hispánica del Cantar de Mió Cid a García Lorca,* 3rd ed. (Madrid: Aguilar, 1967). The sword as a symbol of adolescence, youth, and old age.

SEBOLD, RUSSELL P. "Un David español, o 'Galán Divino': el Cid Contrarreformista de Guillén de Castro," pp. 217–42 of *Homage to John M. Hill. In Memoriam,* ed. Walter Poesse (Madrid: Editorial Castalia, 1968). Castro's Cid, a "David" of the Counter-Reformation, is both a physical and divine warrior in the universal striving for salvation. This is an exceedingly interesting and informative article.

WADE, GERALD E. "The Interpretation of the *Comedia,*" *Bulletin of the Comediantes,* XI (Spring, 1959), 1–6. Asks the question "How authoritatively we, in our time, may be able to interpret a Golden Age *comedia?*"

WEIGER, JOHN G. "Another Look at the Biography of Guillén de Castro," *Bulletin of the Comediantes*, X (Spring, 1958), 3–5. Comments on errors regarding Castro's date of birth, his financial status, and his attitude toward marriage.

——. "Matrimony in the Theatre of Guillén de Castro," *Bulletin of the Comediantes*, X (Fall, 1958), 1–3. Happy marriages depend on age, social status, and the right to choose one's mate.

——. "Forced Marriage in Castro's Theatre," *Bulletin of the Comediantes*, XV (Fall, 1963), 1–4. A discussion of this problem in *Cid I* and four other plays.

——. "Los silencios de *Las mocedades del Cid*," *Hispanófila*, 23 (1965), 1–7. Great silences in Act I, great noises in Act II, and the lack of silence in Act III.

——. "Sobre la originalidad e independencia de Guillén de Castro," *Hispanófila*, 31 (1967), 1–5. Shows how Castro seemingly adapts independence and originality to Lope's concept of the "New Comedy."

WILSON, WILLIAM E. "A Note on Fifteen Plays Attributed to Guillén de Castro," *Modern Language Quarterly*, VIII (1947), 393–400. The data of this article corroborate to a large measure Bruerton's classification of authentic and nonauthentic Castro plays.

——. "*Bigoteras* and the Date of Lope's *El cuerdo en su casa*," *Bulletin of the Comediantes*, VII (Fall, 1955), 29–31. Suggests a date of 1612–1615 for Lope's play.

——. "Two Recurring Themes in Castro's Plays" *Bulletin of the Comediantes*, IX (Fall, 1957), 25–27. A study of the theme, "Rescue by Valiant Unknown," in Castro's early plays.

——. "Guillén de Castro and the Codification of Honor," *Bulletin of the Comediantes*, XIX (Spring, 1967), 24–27. Adds a new "Law," *La ley de amistad*, to Northup's list of the "Laws" of the Code of Honor.

——. "Two Notes on Guillén de Castro," *Hispanic Review*, XVIII (1950), 63–66. A reference to *bigoteras* helps to establish the date of *The Deceiver Deceived*. Also indicates that Castro wrote most of Act II of *The Apple of Discord and the Abduction of Helen*.

——. "The Orthoëpy of Certain Words in the Plays of Guillén de Castro," *Hispanic Review*, XXI (1953), 146–50. Based on a mechanical rather than on a rhythmic count of syllables, this article is of but slight value, and was rightfully criticized by J. H. Arjona in *Hispanic Review*, XXXIII (1965), 387–94.

C. Doctoral Dissertations

KROGH, RICHARD N. "The Growth of Guillén de Castro's Dramatic Technique as Shown by Eight Selected Plays" (University of Washington, 1956). Shows how Castro explored fields of his own rather than following Lope's lead in all respects.

LA DU, ROBERT R. "Honor in the Theater of Guillén de Castro" (University of Washington, 1960). Discussion of the honor code with reference to the king, the *hidalgo*, and woman.

PÉREZ, ELISA. "La influencia del romancero en Guillén de Castro" (Wisconsin, 1932). This careful study contains several useful bibliographies in addition to its information concerning the ballads.

PODOL, PETER. "Criticism of the Honor Code in the Spanish Theatre" (Pennsylvania, 1968). There are brief references to *Count Alarcos* and *The Deceiver Deceived*.

WEIGER, JOHN C. "The Relationship of Honor, *Fama* and Death in the Valencian Drama of the Golden Age" (Indiana, 1966). This dissertation has been discussed in the *Notes and References* to Chapter Four, note 1.

D. Books

CASALDUERO, JOAQUÍN. *Estudios sobre el teatro español* (Madrid: Editorial Gredos, 1962). In the chapter "Primera comedia de *Las mocedades del Cid*" (pp. 45–71), Casalduero gives an excellent detailed study of the structure of the play with its many contrasts.

CASTRO, AMÉRICO. *De la edad conflictiva. I. El drama de la honra en España y en su literatura* (Madrid: Taurus, 1961). In this basic study of the background of the Honor Code in the history and literature of Spain, the distinguished Hispanist stresses the effects of the struggle among the Christians, Jews, and Moslems upon the development of the code.

——. *El pensamiento de Cervantes* (Madrid: Imprenta de la Librería y Casa Editorial Hernando, 1925). In the section "El honor" (pp. 361–83), various aspects of the code of honor are discussed.

CEJADOR Y FRAUCA, JULIO. *Historia de la lengua y literatura castellana* (Madrid: Tipografía de la Revista de Archivos, Bibliotecas y Museos, 1915–1922). Guillén de Castro is discussed in IV, 184–190 of this fourteen-volume set which is poorly arranged and not of great value.

CERVANTES SAAVEDRA, MIGUEL DE. *Don Quijote de la Mancha*, ed. F. Rodríguez Marín, 8 volumes (Madrid: Espasa-Calpe, S.A., 1911–1913). There have been several reprints of this *Clásicos Castellanos* edition.

————. *Obras completas,* ed. R. S. Schevill and A. Bonilla, 18 volumes (Madrid: Imprenta de Bernardo Rodríguez, 1914–1941).

COTARELO Y MORI, EMILIO. *Isidoro Maiquez y el teatro de su tiempo* (Madrid: Imprenta de José Perales y Martínez, 1902). Appendix IV, 574–836 gives a list of plays presented in the theaters of Madrid between 1793 and 1819, with information concerning actors, repertoires, etc.

CURTIUS, ERNST ROBERT. *European Literature and the Latin Middle Ages* (New York: Harper and Row, Publishers, 1963). This translation by Willard R. Trask or the original work should be in the library of every student who plans to do advanced work in Spanish literature of the Middle Ages, Renaissance, or Golden Age. It stresses the continuous influence of Latin literature upon the literature of various European nations.

DÍAZ RENGIFO, JUAN. *Arte poética* (Barcelona: Imprenta de María Angela Martí, Viuda, 1759). An early discussion of Spanish versification, the original edition having been published in 1592.

DURÁN, AGUSTÍN, *Romancero general,* vols. X and XVI of *Biblioteca de Autores Españoles* (Madrid: M. Rivadeneyra, 1849, 1851). A collection of several hundred ballads in a format which leaves much to be desired.

FITZMAURICE-KELLY, JAMES. *Chapters on Spanish Literature* (London: A. Constable and Company, Ltd., 1908). Worthwhile studies of a few types of literature and authors. The Cid is discussed on pp. 1–24.

FLOECK, WILFRIED. *"Las mocedades del Cid" von Guillén de Castro und "Le Cid" von Pierre Corneille. Ein neuer Vergleich* (Bonn: Romanisches Seminar der Universität, 1969). This comparative study of the two plays is reviewed in *Filología Moderna,* IX (1969), nos. 33–34, pp. 160–61; *Bulletin of Hispanic Studies,* XLVII (1970), 258–60 and *Bulletin Hispanique,* LXII (1970), 222–24.

FROLDI, RINALDO. *Il teatro valenzano e l'origine della commedia barocca* (Pisa: Editrice Tecnico-Scientifica, 1962). Discusses the influence of the Valencian dramatists upon Lope de Vega.

GARCÍA VALDECASAS, ALFONSO. *El hidalgo y el honor* (Madrid: Revista de Occidente, 1948). The last two chapters, "Naturaleza del honor" and "El honor español," are especially valuable for a study of honor in the Golden Age.

GREEN, OTIS H. *Spain and the Western Tradition,* 4 volumes (Madison: The University of Wisconsin Press, 1963–1966). This set should be in the library of every person who is interested in Spanish literature from the Middle Ages to the end of the Golden Age.

GUARNER, LUIS. *Romancero del Cid, precedida del Cantar de Rodrigo: Recopilación, prólogo, notas y apéndice* (Valladolid: Miñón, S. A., 1954). Includes the *Cantar de Rodrigo* in Old Spanish and a modern adaptation. The *Romancero del Cid* consists of 189 ballads arranged in chronological order. Five appendices deal with the Cid in modern ballads and the theme of the Cid in French literature.

HÄMEL, ADALBERT. *Der Cid im Spanischen Drama des XVI und XVII Jahrhunderts* (Halle a. S: Verlag von Max Niemeyer, 1910). Deals mostly with the Cid in Golden Age drama plus a short account of the Cid in other types of literature.

HAYES, FRANCIS C. *Lope de Vega* (New York: Twayne Publishers, Inc., 1967). A well-written book which presents information about Lope's life, writings and technique which is not available in any other book written in English.

HESSE, EVERETT W. *Calderón de la Barca* (New York: Twayne Publishers, Inc., 1967). Valuable discussion of Calderón's dramatic art, with summaries and analyses of plays of various types.

HOLLAND, HENRY RICHARD LORD. *Some Account of the Lives and Writings of Lope Felix de Vega Carpio and Guillen de Castro*, 2 volumes (London: Printed by Thomas Davison, Whitefriars, 1817). An interesting comparison of *Cid I* and *Le Cid* by an English Romanticist who could see nothing worthwhile in *Cid II*.

KELLER, JOHN E. *Alfonso X, El Sabio* (New York: Twayne Publishers, Inc., 1967). Interesting account of Alfonso as King and Patron of Arts and Letters, with excellent comments on his various works.

LANCASTER, HENRY C. *A History of French Dramatic Literature in the Seventeenth Century. Part II. The Period of Corneille, 1635–1651*, 2 volumes (Baltimore: The Johns Hopkins Press, 1932). This authority discusses Corneille's *Le Cid* in I, 118–51.

LEJEALLE, L. and DUBOIS, J. *Le Cid* (Paris: Librairie Larousse, 1965). Introduction to and edition of Corneille's *Le Cid*.

MARSHALL, PAULINE. *El caballero perfecto de Alonso Gerónimo de Salas Barbadillo* (Boulder: University of Colorado Press, 1949). The long introduction has valuable comments on early treatises on courtesy and behavior as well as the Golden Age concept of The Perfect Knight.

MARTINENCHE, ERNEST. *La comedia espagnole en France de Hardy à Racine* (Paris: Hachette et Cie., 1900). Interesting comments by A. F. von Schack, who considers Castro's play to be superior to *Le Cid* (p. 214).

MENÉNDEZ PIDAL, RAMÓN. *Cantar de Mió Cid. Texto, gramática y vocabulario. Tercera Parte: Vocabulario* (Madrid: Espasa-Calpe, S. A., 1945). Valuable comments (904 pages) about vocabulary

and the genealogy of persons mentioned in the *Poem*. For most
entries of individual words the Latin etymon is given.

————. *La España del Cid*, 2 volumes (Madrid: Editorial Plutarco,
S. A., 1929). The most complete work available on the Cid and
Spain of his day.

————. *Poema de Mió Cid* (Madrid: Ediciones de "La Lectura,"
1913), volume 24 of *Clásicos Castellanos*. This edition of the
Poem deals with such aspects as its historical background, fictitious elements, and artistic value. The complete *Poem* with numerous notes is included.

MENÉNDEZ Y PELAYO, MARCELINO. *Antología de poetas líricos castellanos*, 14 volumes (Madrid: Librería de Hernando y Compañía,
1899–1916). Volumes VIII–XII include a reprinting of Wolf's
Primavera y flor de Romances as well as the author's comments
on the historical ballads.

MÉRIMÉE, HENRI. *L'Art Dramatique à Valencia, depuis les origines
jusqu'au commencement du XVII⁰ siècle* (Toulouse: Édouard
Privat, Éditeur, 1913). Chapter X, 539–632 and 696–711 deal
with Guillén de Castro's contributions to this important group of
dramatists.

————. *Spectacles et Comediens à Valencia (1580–1630)* Toulouse:
Édouard Privat, Éditeur, 1913. A detailed study of the theater in
Valencia with comments on actors, troupes, repertoires, etc. Short
references to Castro are found throughout the seven chapters.

MONTOLÍU, MANUEL DE. *El alma de España y sus reflejos en la literatura del siglo de oro* (Barcelona: Editorial Cervantes, 1942). The
author acknowledges his indebtedness to several eminent scholars
for his discussion of various "Souls" of Spain—imperial, chivalric,
picaresque, stoic, and mystic.

————. *Literatura castellana* (Barcelona: Editorial Cervantes, 1929).
A rather superficial work on Spanish literature. Castro is mentioned on pp. 646–47.

MOREL-FATIO, ALFRED. *Études sur l'Espagne, Première Série* (Paris:
Librairie E. Bouillon, 1895). Short discussion of Spanish influence
in France in the seventeenth century, pp. 43–60.

MORLEY, S. GRISWOLD. *Spanish Ballads (Romances escogidos)* New
York: Henry Holt and Company, 1938. Collection of ballads of
various types with excellent introduction and notes.

MORLEY, S. GRISWOLD and BRUERTON, COURTNEY. *The Chronology of
Lope de Vega's "Comedias"* (New York: The Modern Language
Association, 1940). Their application of the use of quantitative
data to establish the chronology of Lope's plays has been referred
to as a "highlight" in literary investigation. This book should be
in the library of every serious student of Golden Age drama. A

second and augmented edition was made by Professor Morley in 1968 and published in Madrid by Gredos: *Cronología de las comedias de Lope de Vega.*

NORTHUP, GEORGE TYLER. *An Introduction to Spanish Literature* (Chicago: University of Chicago Press, 1925). Revised by Nicholson B. Adams, 1940. An excellent study of Spain's literature.

————. *Three Plays by Calderón* (Boston: D. C. Heath and Company, 1926). An edition of *Casa con dos puertas mala es de guardar, La vida es sueño,* and *La cena del Rey Baltasar.* Has an excellent study of the honor code and Calderón's style, with numerous notes on each play.

PARKER, A. A. *The Approach to the Spanish Drama of the Golden Age* (London: The Hispanic and Luso-Brazilian Councils, 1957). Five principles which help to analyze Golden Age plays.

PULGAR, FERNANDO DEL. *Claros varones de Castilla,* ed. J. Domínguez Bordona, *Clásicos Castellanos,* 49 (Madrid: Ediciones de "La Lectura," 1923). Discusses important historical figures, including Rodrigo de Villandrando, main character of Castro's *Proud Humility.*

ROATEN, DARNELL H. and SÁNCHEZ Y ESCRIBANO, F. *Wölfflin's Principles in Spanish Drama: 1500–1700* (New York: Hispanic Institute in the United States, 1952). An important contribution to the study of the drama of the Renaissance and the Baroque period.

SAINZ DE ROBLES, FEDERICO C. *El teatro español, historia y antología,* 7 volumes (Madrid: M. Aguilar, 1942–1943). Castro is discussed in IV, 19–25. Included are *Cid I* and *Cid II,* without notes.

SALVÁ, D. PEDRO. *Cancionero de la Academia de los Nocturnos de Valencia estractado de sus actas originales,* ed. Francisco Martí Grajales, 4 volumes (Valencia: Imprenta de Francisco Vives y Mora, 1905–1906). Castro's contributions are listed in IV, 196–197. Biographical material on Castro in III, 119–79.

SÁNCHEZ, JOSÉ. *Academias literarias del siglo de oro español* (Madrid: Editorial Gredos, 1961). Short account of *Academia de los montañeses del Parnaso,* pp. 227–28. A few references to Castro *passim.*

SIMÓN DÍAZ, JOSÉ. *Bibliografía de la literatura hispánica* (Madrid: Consejo Superior de Investigaciones Científicas), 8 volumes to date; VII (1967), 713–34 provides the most complete bibliography available on Castro. Critical comments are lacking.

SOUTHEY, ROBERT. *The Chronicle of the Cid* (New York: The Heritage Press, 1958). This account, written in archaic style, is based on *The General Chronicle,* the *Poem of the Cid,* and the Cid ballads.

TICKNOR, GEORGE. *History of Spanish Literature,* Fourth American Edition, 3 volumes (Boston: James R. Osgood and Company, 1872).

This is the first history in any language of the literature of Spain.

VALBUENA PRAT, ANGEL. *Historia del teatro español* (Barcelona: Editorial Noguer, S. A., 1956). For interesting comments on Corneille's adaptation of *Cid I*, see pp. 127–33.

VEGA, LOPE DE. *Arte nuevo de hacer comedias en este tiempo* (Buenos Aires-México: Espasa-Calpe Argentina, S. A., 1958). Trans. W. T. Bruester. *The New Art of Writing Plays* in *Papers on Playmaking* (New York: Drama books, 1957).

WILSON, MARGARET. *Spanish Drama of the Golden Age* (Oxford: Pergamon Press, Ltd., 1969). An excellent study of the development of the Spanish drama from the early Renaissance to the end of the seventeenth century.

WÖLFFLIN, HEINRICH. *Kunstgeschichtliche Grundbegriffe: das Problem der Stilentwickelung in der neuren Kunst* (München: F. Bruckmann a-g., 1915). English translation by M. D. Hottinger. *Principles of Art History: the Problem of the Development of Style in Later Art* (New York: Dover Publications, 1929).

WRIGHT, C. H. C. *A History of French Literature* (New York: Oxford University Press, 1925). Castro and Corneille are discussed on pp. 305 ff.

Index